IN MEMORIUM

This Book is Dedicated to
GLADYS EDWARDS

who, again and again,
gave away all her substance
and lived out her whole life on this earth
for two who called her "Mom."
She was my all time number one fan
and one of the dearest treasures God
in His merciful providence
ever bestowed on a son.

See you again, Mom
in realms of blazing light
where none can be found
except we be found in God.

REVOLUTION

The Story of
THE EARLY CHURCH

by   GENE EDWARDS

Revolution
Printed in the United States of America
All rights reserved

Published by: SeedSowers
                  P.O.Box 285, Sargent, GA 30275
                  800-228-2665
                  www.seedsowers.com

Library of Congress Cataloging-in-Publication Data

Edwards, Gene
        Revolution /Gene Edwards
        ISBN 0-940232-02-2
        1. Spiritual Life.   1. Title

Times New Roman 10pt

Books by Gene Edwards

Church Life/House Church

How to Meet in Homes
Climb the Highest Mountain
When the Church was Led Only by Laymen
An Open Letter to House Church Leaders
Revolution, the Story of the Early Church

Radical Books for Radical Christians

Beyond Radical
Rethinking Elders
Overlooked Christianity

The First-Century Diaries

The Silas Diary
The Titus Diary
The Timothy Diary
Priscilla's Diary (2001)
The Gaius Diary (2002)

Comfort and Healing for the Inner Man

Healing for Those Who Have Been Crucified by Christians
Letters to a Devastated Christian
Dear Lillian
The Prisoner in the Third Cell
A Tale of Three Kings

The Deeper Christian Life

Living by the Highest Life
The Secret to the Christian Life
The Inward Journey

The Chronicles of the Door Series

The Beginning
The Escape
The Birth
The Triumph
The Return

In a Class by Itself

The Divine Romance
Revolutionary Bible Study

CONTENTS

Preface

This marks the first time ever that the entire first-century *story* has been written out in full. Never before has anyone told the *entire* story. In so doing this also marks the only time a *model* of the first century has ever been created.

What is important about a model of the first century church? Scientists, educators, industrialists, archeologists, medical professionals, economists, manufacturers, historians . . . *all* use models.

Every minister in every Bible school and seminary should be *required* to create a first-century model, thereby showing what he believes happened in Century One. With no model, the minister is free to change his views and interpretations on a whim, usually to justify his actions.

In all, you will find six books telling the complete first-century story: *Revolution, The Silas Diary, The Titus Diary, The Timothy Diary, Priscilla's Diary,* and *The Gaius Diary.**

I urge you to read this story . . . always asking yourself: do the modern-day practices of Christianity bear any resemblance to what happened in Century One?

May our Lord *revolutionize* our understanding of that story, thereby revolutionizing our entire understanding of the New Testament. This, in turn, *must* revolutionize the entire practice of the ekklesia.

Lord, bring on the revolution!

—*Gene Edwards*

---

* Read *The Return*, serves as the dramatic end to the story. It depicts the Lord's return.

The Jerusalem Line

The First Seventeen Years
30-47 A.D.

Jerusalem
Judea
Antioch

1

Two Months Before

In late March and early April of 30 a.d., an uncommonly large number of ships had begun landing at Caesarea and the other seaport towns of Judea. They were packed with passengers who, disembarking, made their way thirty miles inland to the ancient city of Jerusalem. All roads leading to that city were congested with travelers. Not only from the seaports but south from Africa, east from Assyria, and north from Asia Minor and Europe, people were pressing toward the ancient capital of Judea.

First the people came in trickles, then in masses and finally, like a great flood they poured into the Holy City from all points on the compass. The first to arrive filled up the inns. Later all the homes and apartments were taken. Eventually all living quarters were overflowing. Yet still the travelers came until the situation was near chaos. Late arrivers began camping in the streets, and eventually even they were choked with religious tourists.

From all across the known world they came, squeezing and jamming into a city barely one square mile in size.

Every year at this same time, the city of Jerusalem played host to visiting Jews from across the earth who came to celebrate a series of ancient holidays. It was something like a world's fair, a solemn religious pilgrimage, an international tourist attraction and a family reunion all rolled into one. The period of celebrations lasted about sixty days beginning with crop planting. Next came the solemn Passover, then the observance of First Fruits and finally, seven weeks later, a delightful feast called "The Feast of Weeks," or "Pentecost."

The Jews had celebrated this season annually for well over a thousand years. In fact, the year 30 a.d. would be close to the fifteen hundredth celebration of this holiday season.

The typical Jewish tourist had a fairly clear understanding of the Passover ritual as an annual reminder to Israel of a very important promise.

The next great celebration which followed the Passover was known as First Fruits. Its spiritual meaning was much more obscure than that of the Passover celebration. Most Jewish people were aware only that it had to do with the annual planting of grain.

First Fruits was a celebration acted out during crop planting time: if God gave a good planting season, and later a good harvest, it meant a good year for Israel. A poor harvest could mean disaster or even famine.

This celebration was pictured in a ritual enacted *three* days *after* Passover. But it was obvious that the rite of First Fruits also had some deeper and more hidden spiritual significance which was not generally known.

Some tourists left Jerusalem as soon as the First Fruits celebration was over, but many stayed to celebrate Pentecost, observed exactly seven weeks later. The true spiritual significance of Pentecost was much more obscure than the Passover or even First Fruits. No one seemed to understand exactly what future event Pentecost foretold. (Most people in our century do not know either!)

During this particular year another big, but unscheduled, event was taking place. A trial which had everyone talking was also being held in the city. A Nazarite, about whom there were all kinds of rumors, was being tried for His life. Abruptly, He was sentenced to die. His execution was hurriedly pushed through the courts to keep it from interfering with the observance of the main part of the Passover.

It so happened that even while the Nazarite was being cross-examined in court, a group of priests was closely scrutinizing a lamb, getting it ready for the Passover, making sure it was without blemish. The two events, the man's execution and the slaughter of the lamb for the Passover, paralleled one another so closely that, just as the convicted man was led to the hill of execution, the lamb was taken to the temple and prepared for sacrifice.

The next day, Saturday, everyone observed the Sabbath rest. Sunday was coming up, at which time the celebration of First Fruits would take place.

Just before the Sunday morning sunrise one of the temple priests left the temple and made his way toward a field nearby Jerusalem. Once there, the priest carefully inspected the soil to see if any sprouts (first fruits) of seed had broken up out of the ground.

It was still dark. The sun had still not dawned. At least one other person, however, a woman named Mary Magdalene, was also up. She was one of the followers of Jesus, and she was on her way to inspect the grave where *He* was laid.

Sure enough, the priest arrived at the field just as dawn broke and the first rays of morning lit the field before him. As he stooped down at the edge of the field, he could see it! There at his feet a seed had broken ground. A little sprout, a first fruit of that year's crop, had come up!

The priest reached down. His hands carefully enfolded the tiny sprout, and he began to lift it out of the soil. At just that moment, he felt the earth shaking beneath him. (There was obviously a violent earthquake somewhere nearby.) Also at that same moment, the sun broke over the horizon.

The priest quickly lifted the sprout from the ground and carried it back to the temple. There he enacted the ritual of First Fruits. He held the sprout in his uplifted hands before the altar; he stood waving it back and forth before God. He offered the sprouted grain up to God in an ancient rite of thanksgiving that the seed had broken out of the soil.

In the meantime a wild rumor had begun to sweep across Jerusalem. It seemed to have originated with that young girl, Mary Magdalene. She was declaring that when she went to the tomb she found it empty—and that Jesus had come up out of the earth, alive!

It was on this note that the second big celebration, "First Fruits," ended.

In exactly forty-nine days . . . in seven weeks . . . the next great celebration would be observed, no, this time *fulfilled!!* On that day the priest would return to the same field where he had earlier picked a sprout. The grain would have ripened by then and he would collect an armful of wheat. That day, that incredible day, will be the day of Pentecost.

As you can see, some rather unbelievable things happened during the observance of the Passover and First Fruits in the year 30 A.D.

This year's Pentecost wouldn't exactly be business as usual, either!

2

Sunday, 5 a.m. - 8 a.m.

It is Sunday, May 29, 30 A.D. It is about 5:00 a.m. The sun is not yet up. Jerusalem is still dark.

The doors of the temple swing slightly open. A lone priest makes his way through the door, down the stairs, and through the streets of Jerusalem. The streets, as far as he can see in the morning gray, are packed with sleeping pilgrims who lie everywhere on the stone pavement. He threads his way through the slumbering maze, passes through the city gate and out into the open countryside. He is on his way to a nearby field, the same field he inspected exactly forty-nine days ago.

This priest is not the only one out so early. A few other people are also up. A few of the Lord's disciples can be seen carefully working their way through the sleeping crowds, along the narrow city corridors and up the stairs of a two story building. (This building is located quite near the temple area.)

We know what the priest is doing on this particular Sunday morning, but why are over 100 disciples up so early? The answer can be traced back to the Passover and the events of the ensuing forty-nine days. Just a little over seven weeks earlier Jesus Christ had been crucified during the Passover. Just about every one who had been meeting in the upstairs room was an eye-witness to his execution. The two days that followed His execution were the darkest, saddest days these men and women ever lived. The whole experience was crushing—almost beyond human endurance. But forty-nine days ago all this unbearable sorrow was turned into inexpressible joy. Why? Because it was then that Mary Magdalene returned from visiting Jesus' tomb declaring that it was empty. Furthermore, she insisted she had seen the Lord . . . alive!

During the next five weeks the Lord appeared, from time to time, to all these people. On the fortieth day after His resurrection He had a short talk with a small group of them on a hilltop near Jerusalem called the Mount of Olives. At that time He gave His disciples a few words of instruction. He specifically singled out twelve of them, looked them straight in the eye and said, "You are going to receive power." He then told all those who were with Him to go to Jerusalem and wait for the coming of the Holy Spirit. When He had finished giving these brief instructions, He began to ascend from the earth and disappeared into the skies.

The disciples had stood there a moment, dumbfounded. Not one of them knew what, or who, the Holy Spirit was, nor when it, He, would come. But with the few words of instruction they had been given, they all decided to move to Jerusalem, rent a large room where they could meet together and, as the Lord had said, wait. Since they knew nothing else to do, they decided their time would best be spent in fasting and prayer.

It was still dark. Someone began to softly sing a Psalm; others joined in. The most historic prayer meeting in human history was underway!

The temple priest arrived at the grain field just outside the city. The sun's first rays began to spread across the land before him. Seven weeks ago, on the day of First Fruits, this same priest had inspected this same field. Unlike seven weeks ago when only little sprouts had been coming up, now the field was full and rich with a very ripe crop of grain. The seed planted during the Passover season had come up as a high, abundant crop, ready for harvest. The priest stepped out into the field and began cutting some of the stalks. He carefully gathered two bundles, turned, and started back to Jerusalem.

Darkness gave way to day. Jerusalem had begun to stir under the first bright beams of the morning light. The priest re-entered the temple. The next important step of the Pentecost ritual was about to begin.

The priest walked to a table and began to beat the seed from the stalks he had gathered. Next he took a smooth, convex stone and worked it carefully back and forth over the seed. He kept pressing the seed until it was thoroughly crushed. He continued the grinding until the seed was a heap of finely ground flour.

The priest heaped up the finely ground flour. Carefully he poured some water on it and molded it into dough. He fashioned the dough into loaves. He then took the loaves and slipped them into the depths of a fired oven. He stepped back, and waited.

The oven was very hot. Soon the dough would be bread; the priest would soon reach again into the depths of the heat, this time to take the finished loaf out of the oven.

In just a few moments the priest would open the oven door, lift out the loaf, take it to the altar and hold it up before the Lord. That offering would be the high hour of Pentecost—and that very moment was at hand.

It was about 8:00 a.m.

The prayers in the upper room had become awesomely real, and very bold. The presence of the Lord was also very real. Suddenly there was a loud sound. It seemed to be coming from the heavens. It was a mighty, deafening roar. It grew louder and closer.

The room almost rocked under the fury of its blowing. Something incredible was happening. What was it? Was it the life Christ spoke of? The Holy Spirit He promised? The power He promised to give? The kingdom of which He spoke? One thing was sure, something heavenly was about to strike earth.

Then it happened, right there among them. The sound of the wind *from heaven* entered that room *on earth*. That wonderful sense of the reality and the closeness and the presence of Christ, a sense they had only experienced when they sat in His very presence while He was here on earth—that same glorious presence filled the room. Even more, an awesome sense of His divine authority was there.

Suddenly everyone knew!

15

The Holy Spirit had come! The divine breath was there — resting upon every person in the room. The whole room was filled, absolutely filled, saturated, and running over, with the Holy Spirit. The presence of that One enveloped and immersed them all!

There had never been anything like it, not ever! Someone shouted. A cry of unutterable joy went up. Then another. And another. They were expressions of praise and glory to the Lord for what He had done in their midst. But there was no way a human being could give adequate expression to such a moment. Yet everyone had to try. To withhold praise at such a time would have been both unthinkable and impossible. The joy of all the believers blended into one great, rising crescendo of praise.

The priest pulled the loaf from the oven. He took it before the altar and lifted it up to the Lord. The high hour of Pentecost had come. The loaf was complete.

A divine seed had come up! That divine life had once dwelt in only one man; today it dwelt in *more* than *one* man! There was even more to it than that. Those men who had divine life were now all one — one body. But there was still more: the Holy Spirit had come. But there was still more: men had been enveloped and saturated in that Spirit. Yes, but there was more. Is it possible? Could there be more?

Yes!

The priest lifted up the loaf of bread before the Lord. The day of Pentecost had come. No! The day of Pentecost had more than come: the day of Pentecost was fulfilled! The most titanic event in creation's history had finally arrived. The divine purpose for the existence of this universe had at last begun. The highest thought God ever had was at last visible upon earth.

What was it? As of the day, in the city of Jerusalem, the rule and the Kingdom that until then only Heaven had known — at last — invaded the earth. The Kingdom of Heaven touched earth. What an awesome event. At last God's Kingdom had enlarged! It had moved to the offensive. It had taken new territory. A beachhead for the Kingdom of Heaven was established on this planet. It might appear to have been a small beginning, but it was destined to enlarge.

What had happened?

The most awesome event in human history. A seed had become one loaf!

The church was born.

3

Sunday, 8 a.m.

Peter stepped out the door and looked at the scene below him. As far as he could see to the west, the narrow street was jammed with people. Just beside him to the east were the temple grounds, packed with over a quarter of a million people. Only a few moments ago all these people had been moving slowly but steadily toward the temple. But now they had stopped and turned around. Every eye seemed to be looking up at Peter. Every face seemed to be asking for some explanation of what they had just seen.

Peter hurried down the steps and knifed his way through the crowd. He was trying to reach a vantage point from which he could be seen and heard by both the throng of pilgrims in the street and the mass of worshippers already in the temple grounds.

As Peter made his way through the crowd, the rest of the believers in the upper room also spilled out the door and followed him into the street. In a moment Peter reached the edge of the temple yard. He turned to face the crowd. Instinctively, eleven other men threaded their way through the crowd and took their place beside him.

Peter raised his hand. The whole throng fell quiet.

Who is this man Peter? Who are these eleven men standing like a wall at his side? Where did this gigantic audience come from? Why is everyone suddenly so interested in hearing from Peter?

The time is about 8:30 a.m.

The day is Sunday, May 30, 30 a.d.

The people are Jews. They have come from all over the Roman Empire. For weeks they have been on ships, in

19

caravans and on roads, traversing seas and continents to get here. They are tourists. They have travelled to the native land of their forefathers to join in a great annual celebration in this, the capital city. The number of foreigners present in the city today is a mind-boggling 500,000. They have jammed their way into every inch of the one square mile that is Jerusalem. Early this Sunday morning they all left their rooms, inns and pallets on the street and began pouring into the temple area to join the festivities of Pentecost.

This is the very first time that many of these people have seen the Holy City. The visitors are easy to distinguish from the usual 100,000 residents. Most of them speak Hebrew with a thick accent. Their native tongues are Greek, Latin or one of a dozen other languages spoken in the Roman Empire.

It was, in fact, something to do with languages which had caught all these people's attention. All morning, since dawn, the pilgrims had been passing without interruption down this street, past the upper room where the disciples were gathered, and out into the temple grounds. But at about 8 a.m., the procession had come to an abrupt halt. They had heard a faint rumbling sound in the sky. Looking up, they listened and waited. Gradually the sound had grown into an ear-shattering roar—like the sound of wind blowing at hurricane velocity. As they listened they began to realize that the sound was moving earthward. It seemed to be headed for that two-story house right on the edge of the temple grounds. Then the deafening roar actually *entered* the second story room!

No one knew what to expect next. Everyone just stood there, waiting and wondering. Was this the judgment of God? Would the house crumble, perhaps burst into flame? The answer came quickly.

All of a sudden, the most exuberant shouts anyone had ever heard began pouring out the windows of that building. It sounded like a multitude of people up there. (The number was actually 120.)

Every eye was glued to that second story room.

In the next moment the door opened and a man shot out of the room. They would have thought him crazy except his face was aglow. He was praising God at the top of his voice.

20

He began calling down to people in the street, speaking in his native Galilean dialect. Then, to everyone's amazement, he began proclaiming something about the Messiah . . . in *another* language! About that time another Galilean rushed through the door. He was pouring out praises to God in flawless Greek. Soon out came another wild man, flailing away in articulate Latin. Then came another, speaking Egyptian. And another, Persian. More Galileans, more languages! All were praising God and exalting the Messiah. All were announcing something about a Nazarene, Jesus—His death, His resurrection. They were all saying that God had made this Jesus both Lord and Christ!

The people on the street were dumbfounded. No one had ever seen or heard of anything like this. And for a few skeptics in the crowd, it was just a little too much. Somebody just had to yell out, "They're all drunk. That's all it is. They're drunk." The crowd twittered and laughed with relief. At least this was something of a logical explanation for all these strange happenings.

But word of this accusation had meanwhile made its way up to that second story room to the ears of Simon Peter. Instantly he decided to go outside and address the people. He would briefly explain to them that what they were seeing was not just a bunch of happy drunks.

As Peter started out of the room he must have realized that the last few moments were some of the most spectacular and important in all the annals of mankind. History was being made by the minute. Things never before known, heard of or dreamed of were being introduced to this planet. Only a few moments ago the very *Spirit* of the Lord had come down and clothed man! Within the same hour the *Kingdom* of God, a Kingdom that until this time had confined itself to the realm of the heavens, had moved to the earth. Earth had been annexed by the Kingdom of God! But the greatest event of all was this: the *church* had been born!

The planet would never recover from this day. Page one of church history had been written.

As Peter darted down the stairs, still another milestone in God's dealings with man was being reached. At that very moment, *Apostleship* was being born. Apostleship and the church always go hand in hand.

Peter may have been aware of these things as he stepped into the courtyard. But he did not know that he was about to bring the most spectacular message ever delivered by a mortal. Peter was really planning to say very little as he turned to face the crowd, flanked by the other eleven disciples. (No, they were no longer "the twelve disciples;" at this very moment they were becoming "the twelve *Apostles*.")

Just before Peter speaks we would be wise to learn a little more about him. The church is less than an hour old, and it is Peter who is first to step upon the stage of church history. It is with Peter's entrance that the curtain rises on the story of the early church.

As to his place in society, Simon Peter was a commercial fisherman. He was about thirty years old. For most of his life he had had the reputation of a filthy-tongued, joking, shallow, loud-mouthed braggart. He had never read a book in his entire life. He was illiterate. It is doubtful that he could even sign his own name.

A little over four years ago, Peter had been one of the curious who went out in the wilderness to hear John the Baptist. Until then he was only a face in the crowd, destined to be one of the nameless, unknown billions who pass through the annals of time utterly unnoticed.

When Peter listened to John the Baptist, he had fallen under deep conviction. John's words hit him like a hammer. Peter crumbled. Penitent, sorrowful, and awakened to his sin, he turned to the living God.

A few months later Simon had gone out to hear and to meet yet another Prophet—Jesus the Nazarite. Sporadically he followed Jesus around. Finally, entranced by what he saw and heard, he began following the Lord *everywhere,* night and day. He became one of several hundred people who spent all their time following Jesus.

One day Jesus turned around, faced Peter and said, "Follow Me." Jesus was personal and serious. Simon responded: he sold everything he had on earth except the clothes on his back, and he followed the Lord. From that day on, the Lord allowed him into an inner fellowship of less than twenty men.

For the next three and a half or four years, Simon Peter was never out of sight of the Lord. He lived and breathed, ate and slept in the constant presence of Jesus Christ. Such experience greatly altered his life. Nonetheless, Peter proved to be a rather dull, thick-headed disciple. Right up to the time the Lord was arrested, he was either calling down fire on a city or trying to defend with a sword. The denial, the cross, and the three days that followed the crucifixion of the Lord changed all that. Then, at last, Peter was a broken man. After Jesus Christ ascended, Peter and the others spent ten days in constant prayer and fasting. During those ten days, confession and tears gushed from him like a torrent. He was permanently a shamed, humbled and broken man. Peter had finally seen what he was *really* like.

So this was the kind of man who was cutting his way through the crowd. His thoughts were wholly on his Lord. On this day, Simon was simply one crushed, sifted grain, only one small part of a great loaf. Peter was nothing! A meek man would address the multitude.

It was a soft, tenderhearted Apostle who looked out upon that wondering mass of humanity. Peter's face was flushed. His eyes were red and filled with tears. He was certainly not aware that he was setting the standard for all Apostles to come after him. But Peter had been prepared for this moment: John the Baptist, repentance, meeting Christ, following Him, selling and losing all, having nothing, being called and chosen to be an Apostle, nearly four years of living in the Lord's presence, no service, no work, no ministry, no significant "witnessing," just years spent with Christ, then the cross. Then came the prayer, the brokenness and the Holy Spirit. Finally, finally after all this, today he was being *sent* by the Lord. At this very moment he had become "a sent one, an Apostle."

The purpose of an Apostle is to build the church, and Simon Peter was going into the building business.

Dear reader, as the story of the early church unfolds, we will, from time to time, pick up threads that wind their way continuously through this drama. The first thread we run across is given to us by Simon Peter. Apostleship was born in him in the same instant the church was born. Without Apostles the church would never have gotten past gestation.

23

Today Christianity has wandered far afield from the early church. A restoration is needed. Certainly the first thing that needs to be restored in the church is the first thing the Lord ever *gave* the church: Apostles. Without the full restoration of this office, all other discussion, all other hopes, all other dreams and plans of seeing the church again as it ought to be are meaningless.

Therefore, as we watch Peter and the eleven men who stand beside him, let us keep in mind that we are witnessing the genesis of Apostleship, the first secret of the greatness of the early church. The restoration of the church in this age demands, first and foremost, the restoration of this office: the restoring of church planters.

It was about 8:45 a.m. Peter began slowly. "Men and brethren, the people you see here are not drunk, as some of you are saying. It is not even 9 a.m. yet." This concluded Peter's entire planned message. But, even as he made this simple explanation, he noticed that the whole crowd was standing, expectant and silent, wanting some further word. At that moment a thought flashed through his mind. He had told them what all this was *not*. Why not tell them what it was!

Peter proceeded. He began explaining exactly what had taken place in the upper room by quoting Joel, an ancient prophet. Little by little, Peter unraveled the seeming mystery of the morning's events.

Again, he would have stopped, but by this time he was aware that the multitude was hanging on every word. Suddenly something broke in Peter. The message of Christ burst from him in a torrent. For one long moment everyone stood spellbound. His words struck like fully bowed arrows.

Suddenly someone from the vast crowd shouted out, half yelling, half crying, "What must we do to be saved?" The Holy Spirit, so new in His work upon the earth, had moved throughout the entire multitude. There was no one in that throng who had ever had an experience like this, the experience of being convicted of sin by the Holy Spirit. Peter quickly ended his talk. His finish was just as unplanned as his beginning. In one short thunderous sentence that was heard the length and breadth of the whole temple area, Peter roared the answer: "Repent and be baptized in the name of Jesus Christ!" That was all.

Instantly, the other eleven sensed that more should be done. They began moving among the people, exhorting, proclaiming, explaining, declaring, and answering questions in all languages. After all, in a crowd this vast Peter's words could not have been clearly understood by all. Each of the eleven took up a spot in the crowd and began answering questions and proclaiming Christ. As it turned out, all of the twelve shared in the experience of declaring Christ to the limitless throng.

Until now, there had been only one type of follower of Christ: there had been 120 believers in the upper room. But as the eleven moved out into the crowd something new happened. Now twelve of the 120 were unique. Now there were 108 disciples and twelve *Apostles.* The first office in the church was now fully born and fully operating!

As the twelve Apostles proclaimed the Gospel to the thousands of people in the street, the festival was forgotten. The people turned to hear the Apostle nearest them. They were deeply moved. It was evident that God had endowed twelve men with great power: hundreds were being saved through their corporate witness. By the time evening came, some three thousand people had marched together out of the city gates, down to the Kidron River and been baptized.*

It was a wonderful, glorious day, a day of praise, and a day of great joy. There had never been a day quite like it in all of human history. The Holy Spirit had descended from heaven, something heavenly had come to earth. The church had been born in 120 believers. Apostleship had been established. The church had grown, in its first day, from 120 to about 3,120.

*It is possible the site might have been in the city at one of the pools . . . perhaps the Pool of Bethesda.

4

Getting Ready for Monday

The day of Pentecost is over.

Tomorrow is the *second* day in church history.

Tomorrow is the *first* day the church meets.

In a few hours now, the temple grounds will be filling up with 3,000 new converts. Monday. The real beginning of the practice of the church. The twelve Apostles will go out and join that meeting. What will they say? What are their plans?

Undoubtedly, the twelve men must have, though there is no record of it, gotten together to figure out the answer to that question. If they did get together for such a meeting, the results must have been quite an eye opener! The problems they face are so gigantic they almost defy understanding. Sunday had its glory; Monday has its problems!

What were the problems facing the twelve?

First of all they were obviously in the wrong town.

These men were all Galileans; Galilee is the land of country people. But look at them now! Here they are in the great, sophisticated capital city of Jerusalem. They do not belong here. They had come here for no reason except to hold a prayer meeting. They only arrived eleven days ago! They had no thought of *staying.*

Why be here at all? Why don't they go home . . . now?

They will *stay!* They will stay because eleven days ago the Lord told them to stay! And He had a very deliberate reason in selecting Jerusalem. But His command had put them in a mess. Here they are, in Jerusalem, with no money, no jobs, and no place to live. There is no Galilean Sea in Jerusalem for these unemployed fishermen to cast their nets into. Furthermore, this city, of all cities, is not friendly to them. Less than two months ago the local government here sentenced *their* Lord to death. To say the least, they are not liked.

They have a *second* problem. Where will they sleep? Where will they eat? How will they make a living? Most of the 120 had probably been "camping out" in the upper room for the last eleven days. (It is even probable that "living with all things in common" was born right there in the upper room.) How could they begin a new work of God on this earth when they were flat broke and in such a ridiculous predicament?

These were the problems of the *twelve.*

They were serious problems all right, but nothing compared to the problems faced by the rest of the 120. Let's look at *their* problems!

The 120 are also Galileans. They, too, had been following the Lord around for over three years. They, too, own nothing. (They had obeyed the Lord's injunction to drop all and follow Him!) Their homes and jobs, *if* in fact they still have any, are in Galilee. Certainly they have nothing in Jerusalem. Nor do they know anyone in Jerusalem. The 120 are unemployed, broke, and in a hostile city.

So, together, the 120 and the twelve have some very serious problems. But the Apostles and the 120 have no problems at all compared to the 3,000.

They have problems!

You see, most of those 3,000 people should be packing their bags right now. They *should* be getting ready to head back home . . . in caravans and on ships! Most of these 3,000 people do not live in Jerusalem or in Galilee. Nor is Judea their home. The vast majority of the 3,000 live hundreds and hundreds of miles away. They have mountains to climb, deserts to trudge, rivers to forge and seas to cross to get home. Certainly the 3,000 have nothing in Jerusalem!

There is absolutely no reason for them to stay here.

These 3,000 converts had come to Jerusalem just a few weeks ago as pilgrims—tourists—with the idea of staying for a very short time. For many of them the pilgrimage to

Jerusalem was a once-in-a-lifetime event. Like most tourists they had brought just enough money to get them through the festival. As a result, today they have very little left in their pockets; they certainly have *no* jobs; they have no homes; most do not even have a place to sleep tonight; they have very little clothing; at best they have enough food to last for a few days. Simply put, the 3,000 are foreigners, they are a long way from home, they are broke, jobless, and homeless!

Now *that* is a problem!

So you begin to get an idea of the titanic mess the Apostles faced. But this is by no means the end of the list.

Look at this! Here is a church with 3,120 believers and it has no place to hold meetings! Where can you possibly get 3,000 people together in one place in a city of 100,000 people all of whom live in one square mile?

Now you can clearly see what the twelve Apostles were up against. Monday morning had all the makings of a disaster. Obviously there was only one solution to this whole problem: send everyone home and forget the whole thing. A problem this big just has no other solution.

The Apostles could very easily have done this. They could have sent the 120 back to Galilee; they could have told the 3,000 to go on home as planned. That would have been reasonable. But Monday is just not going to be a day to be reasonable. Monday will be a day to be new!! Things never done before in history will be done Monday.

Watch now as the twelve start chopping away at the impossible!

Their first decision is simple: The Lord told them to *begin* in Jerusalem, and in Jerusalem they are determined to begin.

One problem down.

Next was the problem of *where* to meet.

In a city this crowded, where would the Apostles be able to find a place big enough to hold 3,120 people? Amazingly, there *was* an answer. There was one place big enough . . . and it was available. There was a place in the temple courtyard which was *behind* the temple building. When you walked around back of the temple you saw a large roof jutting out from the back wall. This huge shed was in a rather out-of-the-way place—altogether an ideal place to meet. True, it was "open-air" on three sides, and everyone would have to sit on the ground, but it *was* a place to meet. (This huge, roofed-in area had a name; it was referred to as "Solomon's Porch."*)

That still left the biggest problem of all! What would the 3,000 do?

Soon the church was about to have its first meeting in all history! Would the Apostles tell the 3,000 people to stay in Jerusalem? Dare these twelve men tackle the colossal problem of taking on nearly 3,000 homeless, jobless, penniless displaced persons? If they do, if they tell the 3,000 to stay in Jerusalem, and if in a moment of madness the 3,000 take them up on it and stay . . . it will be a most staggering decision. Three thousand people would, in that one day, cut all ties with their families, homes, jobs, friends, ambitions, dreams . . . everything! In one day they would go from security to poverty, from "having" to the "loss of all things." That would be quite a day! Would the twelve have the audacity to ask 3,000 people to do such a thing? What a standard they would raise for all centuries to follow if they do! What a way to *begin*!

If they did ask such an outlandish thing, would the 3,000 ever agree?! It is unthinkable that 3,000 people would say "yes" to such an idea.

To give you some idea of just how far fetched and unlikely the idea is, imagine it this way. Let's say that Pentecost took place in your lifetime. Let's say it took place *yesterday*. If twelve men you never met before in your life asked you, *today*, to sell everything on earth you possessed and take part in some kind of a new organization of sorts called *church*, would you do it? You have to admit that, at best, it would be a rather far out idea. One thing is sure: the

---

*The exact shape and appearance of Solomon's Porch is not certain. It may have been a roofed-in area at the point where two of the courtyard walls came together as a corner. Anyway, it appears that it was on the back side of the temple area, a place not often frequented by temple traffic.

twelve men would be crazy, in our age, to think that "church" was ever going to have very many "takers."

Anyway, by what right would these twelve men presume to ask 3,000 people—all perfect strangers—to do such an insane thing as sell houses, land, property . . . all they have . . . and then agree to abject poverty?

Do not underestimate these men. They *are* Apostles.

They had once been told to sell all and follow the Lord. They obeyed completely . . . and never batted an eyelid. Don't be sure they won't try the same thing with the 3,000. Yes, they still had very vivid memories of that *first* beginning and all that it demanded.

There is more evidence than this that they just might dare such a suggestion.

Don't overlook the influence of the 120. They have already divested themselves of everything. Furthermore, for quite some time now, they have all been piled in together in the upper room. Throughout all the first century, there was always the witness of the 120 to remind other believers what it was really supposed to be like to be a follower of Jesus Christ. They were a living witness to *utter abandonment.* They stood there, a mute testimony that the idea of leaving all to follow Christ was not *totally* insane.

Of course there was still another witness to this. Jesus Christ had lived this way while he was on the earth!! Part of the training of the twelve was the Lord's own example of total disinterest in outward things.

And there is one more thing!

On top of all the other preparation the Lord has put them through, Jesus Christ has also armed these twelve men with the most powerful weapon in history. And, for the first time, they are about to unleash it. The Apostles are about to uncork the *Gospel of the Kingdom!*

Monday morning is about to dawn. Church history is about to begin in earnest.

The twelve will soon be making their way to the temple courtyard. When they get there the place will be teeming with people. Undoubtedly, the first called meeting of the church will be a glorious meeting. At some moment in that meeting the time will undoubtedly come for the twelve to make their plans known. Unquestionably it will be Peter who will drop the bomb.

Hold on to your chair because here it comes!

5

Monday!

What a sight!

The first meeting of the church in history. Three thousand people pouring into Solomon's Porch. Three thousand joyous, expectant faces!

It was undoubtedly in this meeting the Apostles dropped their bomb. They had decided to stay in Jerusalem. Furthermore it was their feeling that all 3,000 of the new converts should stay here, too! The Gospel of the Kingdom was fired at point blank range!

The response was immediate, unbelievable, overwhelming and unanimous. All 3,000 elected to stay!

Working out the details would be staggering . . . if not downright impossible; but for the moment it was a simple, fantastic, insane, glorious decision. In all church history there has really been nothing quite like that moment!

Without homes, beds, shelter, jobs, money or meals, over 3,000 people had decided to drop everything to gain the depths of the riches of knowing Christ. How they would do it without starving, no one knew . . . nor did they care. Their hearts were set. They would *know* the Lord.

It was a most glorious hour.

Only one very simple problem remained to be worked out. Where would everyone sleep that night, where would they eat tomorrow, how would they get food, how—in general—would they survive?

A solution, of sorts, was forthcoming.

There were a few people among the 3,000 who actually did live in the city of Jerusalem. These few people volunteered to open their homes to the rest of the 3,000.

That is where it all began!

(Since we do not really know exactly how many homes there were, let us imagine there were about fifty houses altogether . . . to share among 3,000 people. This means 60 people for every home!)

Of course that meant that in the next few days an awful lot of people slept on the streets, but at least everyone was near a kitchen . . . in case food might somehow become available!

This was just like the situation with the 120 when they came into Jerusalem, rented a big room, and all piled in together . . . only this time it was 3,000!

You can imagine 3,000 people flooding into—and around—about fifty homes. Undoubtedly someone got the idea of moving all the furniture out of the house to leave the floors completely bare so more people could be inside. So out went the furniture! It was probably at this point some dear saint made a simple but revolutionary suggestion that started an amazing series of events. (Or perhaps this action was taken as a result of the Apostles' instructions. These men were not timid about using their authority.) Someone probably got the idea of selling all of that now-useless furniture to buy food. Immediately this practice was taken up in every house. Everyone who had homes in Jerusalem began selling *all* their belongings!

In rapid succession (it appears) someone who owned his own house came up with this next idea. "My home is paid for. I can sell it, take the money, *rent three* homes *and* buy food!" Soon all the Jerusalem believers were selling not only furniture but also their homes and property. (After all, Jesus had made it clear that men would give up houses and lands in the process of gaining His Kingdom.)

If you find it hard to believe that men would do such things, then you have never been in the flood-tide joy of church life. Whether the Apostles suggested it or it began spontaneously, it was an outward expression of an inward joy. Things like losing all became so easy to do, so normal, and so wonderful that they did not even seem unusual.

Now look where that left the *world's* understanding of *Christ!* Look where that left the world in its understanding of the *church*. Look at the image of "church" through the eyes of a typical unbelieving Jerusalem citizen! To anyone on the outside looking in, to be a follower of Christ meant the loss of *all* things: right down to the clothes you wore. Jesus had uniquely made a demand on His followers no other man had ever made. Now the church was born, and it was born obeying that demand. And since the day Jesus Christ made that demand, He has never countermanded it. The demand has not changed even though the practice *has*!!

Do you realize what this means? It means that during the first eight years of church history, to be "in the church" a man knew he would have to deliberately go out and sell everything on earth he had, even become penniless. This was the privilege (the *privilege* mind you) of being "in church!"

That is the image the church bore throughout the whole first century. To become a believer, to be in the church, to lose everything, were all one and the same. That is what it meant to be in the church in Jerusalem. That is what it ought to mean to be in the church today. It is high time she got her proper image back!*

In the midst of tidal joy, men laid down all because of their simple, overwhelming love for Christ. And the love grew out of their experience with Him! By now all 3,000 were getting involved in this "sell everything" experience. The 3,000 who once lived in other cities and other countries began writing back home to have their houses, goods and land sold.

By this amazing abandonment of all things, a dent was made in the "housing and food" problem. Enough money to buy food started to come in. Soon there was enough money to rent more homes! *Eventually* enough houses were rented to get everyone off the streets. And during this same time everybody started looking for jobs. They took any kind of job available. First one, then a few dozen, began finding jobs.

Now something else new began. The people with jobs did not keep their wages. Instead they converted their wages into grocery money for everyone.

*Some of us would probably have refused to become Christians if the standard of church life today were as high as it was in Jerusalem in 30 a.d. Again, would you, right now, be willing to do what they did?

This was sort of makeshift. Someone got the idea of turning their money and property *all* over to the Apostles themselves, to spend the money where most needed! Instead of everyone going out and renting houses and buying food harem-scarem, everyone put everything in a common pool. The money from wages, plus the money which came in from the sale of furniture, houses, land, etc., was all put into one big pile. The Apostles then bought food to meet everyone's basic needs.

Notice who controls the money. Also notice who is least interested in money. (In the years to come, as men retold the story of those glorious, hectic hours, they would say, "We held all things in common, and distributed according to need;" but, in fact, the whole thing started more or less unplanned and spontaneously and sort of grew from there.)

In our century, some men have said this way of living, having *all things in common*, is the way the church was *always* supposed to live. Not so! The church in Jerusalem fell into "all things common" without forethought. Years later, the Jerusalem believers probably returned to a more "normal" way of living. Some churches that were raised up later did not pool all goods and live out of a common pot! Nonetheless, something important happened in Jerusalem. A lot can be said in favor of this wonderful experience of living in common.

First of all, God used these wild, ridiculous circumstances to smash rituals, rip apart customs, destroy social and cultural taboos, and—in general—produce a glorious, all new atmosphere in which to give birth to this revolutionary thing called the church. You might say middle class values were smashed, Jewish mores wrecked, and the "Hebrew way of life" demolished! The church was born free from all national customs and individual preferences.

The church was born in total newness. The importance of this cannot be underestimated. Living in common helped usher in this newness. The church's conduct was "shocking." The church cut its teeth on doing the radical. It had its beginning in being practical, not conventional. The conforming element in men was dealt a mortal blow. The very birth of the church smashed all past concepts man had ever held toward "religion" in any form! "The church" had an expression, and that expression did not look like anything "religion" had ever seen in all world history. When fifty to 200 people pile into one house, all the things usually known to religion, such as ritual, form, pattern, reverence, etc. are smashed! Add the joy of Jesus Christ, stir, and you are well on your way to the foretaste of experiencing the church!

Secondly, this radical new beginning—touched off by living in common—set a very, very high standard of what it meant "to be *in* the church." A certain flavor permeated the whole first century church because of what happened in Jerusalem during those first days. This unique beginning mothered a church that was unorthodox, informal, rambunctious, daring, elastic and glorious. It also cost you an arm and a leg to have anything to do with it. No. It cost you *everything!*

Thirdly, God used these hilarious, ridiculous circumstances to give birth to something called "church life."

And what, exactly, is church life? Church life is something which was experienced by all believers of the first century. (That is, church life was experienced in every city where the church was ever raised up.) This unique experience, this daily out-living of the church, was the major secret of these people. Though not all the churches of the first century "held all things common," all the churches *did* experience the indescribable glory of *church life.* And that unique experience, that wonderful new life style, that indescribable "corporate experience" had its beginning right here in Jerusalem. Church life was born when a bunch of believers, half out of their minds with joy, gave up all they owned and piled into a few houses and started living together. So the experience of the church, this thing called "church life," was born in the *homes* of Jerusalem.

Church life is hard to explain. You *have* to experience it! But know this, dear reader, God never intended you to be His follower *without* it. The life of a believer was never intended to be experienced alone. You were meant to know Christ in a corporate situation. Being a follower of Christ just does not work without church life. God never intended for you to be a follower of Christ except in the context of the experience of church life. The Lord's life does not even work—nor did God intend it to—except as it is experienced corporately. (No wonder the "victorious life" does not work! The "victorious life," the "faith life," the "empowered life," the "spirit-filled life," the "faith-rest life," the "inner light life," the "positional truth life," none of these work. Can't! Jesus Christ only begins to make sense when you know and experience Him in the vital, overwhelming encounter of *church life!*)

Finally, no one need point out to you that there are no steeples, pews, pulpits, stained glass windows or the like, to be found in all this. There is no property, no headquarters, no pastors, no salaried staff workers. Furthermore they were doing very well without all these things, thank you.

Look around! What is the church made up of? There are (1) twelve Apostles, (2) three thousand people, (3) a huge shed, and (4) an awful lot of homes, *plus* a lot of self-giving and a lot of unleashed joy. *This* was the church. And Christ was real. He was being experienced.

Know this: such things are still possible today . . . 2,000 years later. They are supposed to be part of *your* inheritance when you meet Christ.

Now let's see something else just as spectacular and just as breathtaking. Let's go visit a *meeting.* Let's see "a day in the life of the church" . . . first century style.

6

A Day in the Life of the Church

The first rays of sunlight fall on one of the homes where the disciples live together. "A day in the life of the church" is about to begin.

The whole house, even the living room, is packed wall-to-wall with saints! As dawn steals into the room, someone is beginning to awaken; he drowsily turns over, opens his eyes and, just a few inches away from his nose, sees the sleepy grin of another believer. The two blink at one another for a moment, and then the absurdity of the whole surrounding scene begins to dawn upon them. They smile at each other, and the joy of the Lord begins to well up within them. Then both chuckle and quietly whisper, "Praise the Lord," or "Blessed be the God of Israel." Similar refrains of praise and laughter soon answer from all over the room. Within a few moments the whole house is alive with the praises of sleepy-faced but smiling disciples. By the time everyone is up and the bedding put away, the entire neighborhood is swelling with shouts, praises, singing and joy.

Prayers of every conceivable variety find their way to heaven.

By this time, some *sisters* (yes, that is what they were called in those days!) from a neighboring house arrive and help start the morning meal. Other saints are busy straightening up the house and meeting other needs of the moment. Shortly, breakfast is eaten to the accompaniment of singing, laughing, shouting, and praising.

Those who have jobs start off to work, but they get a royal send-off as they step out into the street. The last thing they hear as they trudge off is the fervent exhorting and encouraging of their brothers and sisters. Brothers who do not have jobs will spend a good part of the day looking for one, and/or tending to some of the practical needs of the others. (Everyone, in fact, has a job of some kind, if not for pay, then they just naturally pick up some responsibility in church life . . . *and* keep looking for employment. No one used living in common as a cover for loafing.) The job-seekers get the same glorious send-off as did the employed group. Those who remain at home soon finish the house cleaning and are then off to Solomon's Porch.

As they leave the house and file into the streets, immediately they run into other believers from other houses, headed for the same place. Soon they are trooping through the street together, praising the Lord. All the believers spent as much time as possible sitting in Solomon's Porch listening to the Apostles. During those ancient days a man's life was not yet so systematized by the time clock: there were no eight hour shifts, or formalized work schedules, no punch cards. Therefore, many people who had full-time or part-time jobs could leave their work at odd times during the day and go to Solomon's Porch to catch part of a meeting.

As the happy believers move along the narrow street, they spontaneously break into song; and as they draw closer to the temple grounds, others begin pouring out of houses along the way to join them. Soon these little streams flow together into a river of shouting, singing, excited, expectant disciples.

The rest of the citizens of the city just stand there, shaking their heads in wonder as the rejoicing crowd sweeps by. Outwardly the observers are poo-pooing such childishness, while inwardly many wonder at these people and half wish they could know such an uninhibited feeling of freedom and joy.

Let's join this happy throng and follow them into Solomon's Porch. Let's see "a day in the life of the church" . . . first century style.

As you join the believers for the next sixteen hours, you will be in two meeting places, for two very different purposes. The early churches had a very distinct *tendency* to have two completely different places to meet. (Tendency is the correct word. There was nothing about the early church that was dogmatic. It defied neat categories and rules; it only had *tendencies.*)

The *first* meeting place of the church, the one you are about to enter, is Solomon's Porch. Here the Apostles will be in charge. The *second* place the church meets is in ... no ... wait! Keep your eyes open and see if you can figure out where the second meeting place is. Be careful: the meeting itself is so informal you may never know you are in it!

Why two separate meeting places? A close look will give the obvious answer.

In this first meeting place, that is Solomon's Porch, the Apostles will obviously be leading. That is the main distinction of those particular meetings. Furthermore, the Porch meetings are super-charged and glorious in every way. The second time you gather with the church today, the main thing you will notice is that the meeting, unlike the Porch meeting, is led by absolutely *no one*! That meeting will be completely informal, and it too will be glorious. It will have another distinction: it will be a much smaller meeting; that small, informal gathering will be under the direct leadership of Jesus Christ.

Now let's go in to Solomon's Porch.

The first sight that meets your eyes as you round the corner is that of 3,000 beaming smiles on 3,000 happy faces. Everyone is sitting around on the ground underneath the shed.

We can only imagine what these meetings must have been like.

At times, the whole assembly must have been in awe and wonder as the believers heard of the unfathomable wealth which they had inherited in Jesus Christ. Never had those young followers dreamed that they had a Lord so rich and so immeasurable. Their inheritance in Christ was absolutely breathtaking. At other times, the whole place must have rocked with laughter as the Apostles illustrated some all-too-well-known human frailties. Sometimes, as the new believers began to perceive the greatness and the worthiness of their Lord, they must have broken out into expressions of shouting and joy that made the very earth shake. At other times they must have wept. At other times they must have fallen on their faces and, in stunned awe, worshipped Him with all their being. Then there were times when they sat in rapt attention, soberly considering the demands which their

41

faith required of them. At yet other times, they must have been childlike with glee as they realized that they now belonged to a nation, to a kingdom, which no one else could even see! At still other times, the place must have rolled like an ocean with waves of intense prayer. At other times it was prayer so quiet, so soft, so private you could hardly hear it.

In other words, there was an infinite variety in those meetings. No two meetings were alike and all of them were glorious!

Sometimes one Apostle spoke, sometimes several, and sometimes all of them shared the riches of Christ. Frequently the message would be addressed to the whole throng. At other times they probably broke up into twelve groups and one Apostle met with each group. All day long the scene at Solomon's Porch was that of saints coming and going. Those who had jobs would join the meeting briefly and return to work; others stayed for the whole day!

Possibly there were breaks for meals, rest periods, and times of prayer. Just about anyone, no matter what his work schedule, could get in on some part of a meeting at the Porch.

It goes without saying that those meetings in the Porch looked like nothing you attend during the twentieth century.

Could you possibly imagine these people coming in to *those* meetings, being handed a mimeographed bulletin with a printed "order of worship" on it! Could you see them, day after day, week after week, follow the ritual of three songs, a prayer, another song (then the offering plates!), then some "special music" (some very skilled musician playing on a harp, maybe?) and finally a twenty-five minute message by the Right Reverend Apostle Matthew!

Furthermore, there was no set schedule for the meetings each week (i.e., Sunday morning worship service, eleven a.m.; Wednesday night prayer meeting; Friday night scroll study!) To set a schedule for the church? Impossible! To *know* what the church would do *next* week? To know ahead of time when, where and exactly how you would be meeting for a whole week!? To know that *every* Wednesday would be for prayer meetings! Unthinkable! What a drag! No one knew what would happen tomorrow. No one even had such a ridiculous idea as that of *planning* tomorrow's schedule. That's one reason you went to a meeting: It was the only way to know what would happen next.

When the church is really the church, it is too alive, elastic and on-going to follow a locked-in schedule week after week. Such things just give way when the life of the church and your own daily life are one and the same.

It was exciting to be in the church. Exciting and unpredictable.

It can be that way again, in our day.

While we are here, take a close look around. There are many people in this gathering you will be meeting again as this story unfolds.

For instance, over there sits a young man named Stephen. He comes to every meeting, sitting almost dumbfounded at what he hears, never missing a word. Not too far from him sits a man named Joseph-Barnabas, a new convert who is determined to match everything he hears with a total commitment to his Lord and utter obedience to His word. (We do not know the age of these two men, but let us guess, for future reference, that Stephen is twenty-five and Joseph-Barnabas is thirty.) Look around, and all over the grounds you can see young men who are giving their lives completely to this shaky new enterprise, *the church.*

The heart of every man present is filled with a passion for his Lord. But, like most of us, each one of these men is also filled with a mingled sense of expectation and frustration. Everyone of them has looked at his own inabilities, his weaknesses, and his mixed-up life. Each has wondered how he, such poor material, could ever be a part of the Kingdom of Christ. At the same time, each man would get a glimpse of the greatness of his Lord, and then once more believe against belief that Jesus Christ could transform *even* him! They believed, against themselves, that Christ's life was powerful enough to live in place of their own lives.

The names of some other young men in Solomon's Porch today are Philip; James, the brother of Jesus Christ; Simeon, with his wife and two sons, Rufus and Alexander; a very zealous young convert named Silas; and an intense young man named Agabus, an unlikely seeming candidate for the

Kingdom of God. In the crowd you can also see a very young boy named John-Mark.

Yes, you will very definitely be hearing from these men again, but it will be a *long time*. Repeat: a long time. Despite the fact that Pentecost just ended, absolutely *no one* is going anywhere. No one will go anywhere for the next eight years! Not even the Apostles! Absolutely *no one* has struck out to preach the gospel to the whole world. (Consider that!) Contrary to twentieth century propaganda, Pentecost was *not* the beginning of a drive to evangelize the world!

Unlike our age, these men are not going through seminary or summer orientation, to be shipped out to evangelize the globe. It will be nearly ten years before *any* of these men have any kind of responsibilities in the church. Right now their responsibility is this: to simply, daily, experience the life of Christ with their brothers and sisters. (It will be interesting to note how powerful these men will become *simply* as a result of *experiencing* Christ and *experiencing* His church.) When we meet these men again, years from now, they will not be uncertain young men, but towering giants. Right now, though, they are just new converts *joying* in their salvation, drinking up church life, sitting at the feet of Apostles (under whom they are learning the meaning of authority), and experiencing Christ.

By the way, never once in all of the history of the first century church did men ever receive any kind of special "training for the ministry" such as they do today: i.e., theological seminaries. Greek philosophers did. Jewish priests did. But the Lord's people didn't. Then how did God raise up men? Men of God were prepared just by being in church life. This proved to be all they ever needed! In the church those men got more training, and better training, than *anyone* in the twentieth century has ever received. You simply cannot top church life for preparing servants of God. The Lord never had any other way in mind. The church is His way to raise up His servants.

The 3,000 learned so much in those meetings. At the very same time that they were getting practical help, they were also learning revelation of the deepest spiritual truths. The practical, the spiritual, both were there. The Jerusalem believers were gradually being equipped to live as a *corporate* body and, at the same time find their *individual* ways of expressing their own experiences of Christ.

Have you ever considered just how much those young men received? First of all they sat at the feet of, not theological professors, but Apostles. (Apostles, not seminary professors, are who young men called of God are supposed to sit under!) Secondly, consider the staggering amount of ministry which came from those twelve Apostles. Consider, at the end of eight years, just how much those young men had heard!

Now here is a fascinating question: if you had been sitting there in Solomon's Porch with the 3,000, what would you have heard from the lips of those twelve men? Or, turn it around, if you had been one of the twelve what would you have talked about?

Hold onto your favorite idea because the real answer is a shocker. What they talked about in those meetings rips to shreds just about any twentieth century ministry you have ever been exposed to.

First let's see what those twelve men *didn't* talk about.

They did not get up and deliver sermonettes on being kind to people, or not sinning, or being good. That is obvious.

But you can also bet your favorite doctrine they didn't get up and teach creeds either. They didn't dish out doctrinal statements on every subject in the Hebrew scrolls. In fact, there would be no serious effort at systemizing or categorizing the teaching and doctrines of these men until over 100 years after Pentecost. (And the church would be better for it, if such had *never* happened.) So the first century church had to limp along on a very fluid, very living reality and not on systematized beliefs.

You can also be sure that the favorite topics of today's Christianity were never heard in Solomon's Porch: that is, how to pray, how to witness, how to be victorious over sin, how to study the scrolls, etc.

Of course *everyone* knows what those men were doing up there. They were teaching the Scripture! Why, they were doing what every man of God does. They were getting men into the Word. *Everyone* knows *that.*

Nope!

The Apostles *did not* teach the Scripture.

"You're kidding!"

Nope!

Furthermore, it is unlikely that *any* believers in the first century ever sat around studying the Scripture! Certainly not in the way men do today.

(Undoubtedly you can find a verse somewhere to justify men standing before an audience teaching the Scripture. But in all the story of the first century church you will never once see such a thing as "Bible study" being practiced. Perhaps a verse of Scripture, taken out of context and taken out of its historical setting, can justify such a practice, but the whole story of the early church—if taken from start to finish—simply refuses to endorse such a practice!)

Here are the facts. Approximately eighty percent of the people who lived in the Roman Empire could *not* read or write! So at least eighty percent of the believers of the first century couldn't possibly have studied the Scripture. Add to this the fact that the overwhelming majority of believers were from among the poor, almost none of whom could read, and the percentage of illiterates in the first century church goes even higher.*

Today well over 90% of the followers of Jesus Christ can read, yet it would be fair to say that 99.999% of that score of believers have no idea of how to walk in a deep *experience* of Christ.

Of course, in addition to that, the first century had no printing presses. Do you realize what that means? All copies of Scripture were made by the agonizingly painful, incredibly

---

*The idea that Bible study is an absolute necessity to the Christian Life is so entrenched in the mentality of the twentieth-century believer that to question it is almost an invitation to be burned at the stake. Nonetheless, the fact remains that the early church got by very well without ever engaging in Bible study . . . twentieth century style. This fact is indisputable!

slow, and terribly expensive process of hand copying. A city was fortunate if it had *one* complete copy of the sacred Hebrew writings! Furthermore, about the only place that Scripture was available was in the synagogues—and those synagogues simply were not all that excited about making their scrolls available to followers of Jesus Christ!

It is an indisputable fact that in every place the early church met it had virtually no access to Scripture. No, dear reader, those Apostles weren't standing up there teaching Bible studies for eight years. (In fact, some of them couldn't read either!) Nor will you find the 3,000 sitting around, later in the day, in little Bible study classes.

But none of these facts is the real reason the Apostles did not spend their time teaching the Scripture. If there had been no illiteracy, if there had been an abundance of Scripture, if the Apostles had all been educated men, they still would not have spent their time teaching the Scripture.

To expect those men standing in Solomon's Porch to be teaching the Hebrew scrolls would be like expecting the first man to land on Mars to return to earth and, for his first press conference, to give a lecture on rocket fuel!

The idea of teaching the Scripture never entered their minds!!

The twentieth century mentality alone has superimposed such an image on those men.

They didn't hang up some long wall chart and give lectures on the Scroll of Ezekiel or on "Eyeballs and Bears Tails in the Scroll of Daniel." What is more, the saints gathered in Solomon's Porch would have thrown olive pits at the Apostles if they had tried. The believers had poured into that shed to hear one thing and one thing only. And the Apostles were interested in talking about one thing and one thing only.

What was that?

You can answer that question yourself. If you could go back to that day and be a new convert, and if you could actually sit at the feet of the original twelve Apostles, what would you want to hear?

Or put it another way. If you had just spent four years, eighteen hours per day, living with God, what would you talk about?

The twelve Apostles talked about Jesus Christ! Night and day. That's all you got out of them: Jesus Christ. They originated the whole idea of the *topic* of Jesus Christ, hence the gospels. They couldn't have thought of anything else to talk about if they had tried.

The cutting-edge of today's Christianity is "know the Scripture." This idea virtually enshrouds today's thinking. It is the first and the main thought introduced to all new believers. This all-dominating idea has held first place for the last 200 years—long enough to have been tested and to have brought forth the fruit it is supposed to have produced.

Dear reader, if you ever *really* get to know the Lord in a deep, abiding experience, it will suddenly dawn on you that teaching doctrines was something invented by men who just didn't know the Lord all that well. Men who really know Christ well, will talk about Christ. Men who don't . . . they teach all sorts of interesting, unimportant things. May you be a man who daily, deeply, profoundly meets and experiences the Lord. Then you'll talk about the same thing the Apostles did.

In the first century, the cutting-edge of the faith was to know and experience *Christ.* You can judge for yourself which of these two God honors the most.

That brings up a third fascinating question. What is the secret of the "victorious life?" What did the Apostles say to the 3,000 on this subject?

The answer to that question is virtually unknown today, even undreamed of, among the Lord's people.

Let it be enough for the moment to say that the Apostles talked about their experience of Jesus Christ; and in that subject alone is the secret of the "victorious life." And the 3,000 thrilled at what they heard.

The revelation which the Apostles had of their Lord, their practical help on how to know Him, thrilled every listener and held him in awe of the wonderful adventure that lay ahead.

As night begins to fall and the last meeting is over, the throng breaks up and the saints begin to pour out into the streets to make their way back home.

Let us trudge along with them, for the joy of this day has not yet ended.

Leaving Solomon's Porch and walking along the streets, the disciples praise and sing and chatter, hardly able to contain the glorious things about the Lord which they discovered today. When at last they arrive home they joyfully greet those they live with. It had only been this morning that they said goodbye to one another, yet they all greet each other wildly. It has been eight *whole* hours! So much has happened today! Everybody begins talking at once. Testimonies are exchanged, intermingled with shouts and praises. Everybody is trying to tell everyone else what they have heard, seen and felt. All their talk and joy is centered around one thing: what they experienced *today*. Their sharing is open, natural, and pure. And why not? After all, the people they are sharing with are the dearest people on earth . . . *these* are the people they live with.

Supper is prepared to the accompaniment of uproarious singing, chattering, and laughter. After the meal is prepared, everyone sits down somewhere on the floor to eat and they continue to share. The air is filled with bursts of overflowing life. They testify, praise, and sing. All the experiences of the day, mingled with the joy of the present moment, fill the room. The whole place is saturated with the Lord's presence. Finally the meal comes to an end. Someone spontaneously brings out some bread and wine. The bread is broken, the wine is passed. Once more praising, joy, and more singing ascend.

As the night grows on, the bedding comes out again, and everyone falls asleep to the sound of laughter and joyful praise.

Did you realize you have just been to a *"meeting" of the church!* From the time they got home until they went to bed, *the church was meeting!!* Yes, this was the *second* place the church met. The *main* place the church met was in homes! The meeting, as you have seen, was *totally* informal. Like twelve men sitting around talking with the Lord!

Behold! The church had learned from the twelve how to meet the way the twelve had "met" when they were with the Lord. They met with Him, yet were not even conscious it was a *meeting!* That embryonic "body life" the twelve knew with Christ was now known by all! Those "meetings" (which weren't really meetings at all) which twelve men had while living with Christ, had now become the way the whole church met! The home meetings were to the church what sitting around with Christ had been to the twelve.

Please keep in mind that although on this night there was only one church in Jerusalem, it met in homes all over the city. These home groups did not represent different factions or splinter groups. They were not even groups of favorites or friends meeting together. All the believers, in all the homes, together were *the church,* united, one, in love, inseparable, and glorious.

The church meeting in homes was *one* of the secrets of the early church. Meeting in homes, under Christ, in the midst of unbridled joy was one of the things which makes the church so unique, so wonderful, so believable, and so magnetic. (She must go back there again in order to be what God intended her to be, and she must meet without any human leadership in those meetings!) This is how the church looked when she met during the first century! These are the ways believers met nearly 2,000 years ago: meeting under a shed! Meeting in homes! (That is where she must return . . . utterly forsaking forever the professionally built coffin she now meets in.) Every believer has the inherent right to be in at least one meeting of the church, in a living room, with no human "leader" looking on to ruin it all, in the midst of unrestrained joy. It is an experience for which a substitute is impossible to find.

This was the place the first church met.

Another normal day in the life of the church in Jerusalem has come to an end.

And if God be merciful, those who have the heart will yet see such days again!!

7

Church Life in Modern Dress

Let's imagine for a moment that Pentecost took place in the twentieth century! Let's take the story you just read in the last chapter, and put it in a typical American setting.

To begin, picture a modern, medium-sized city. It is typical in almost every way with the one distinction of being a well-known convention center. Once per year it hosts a famous, international festival which attracts people from all over the world. Otherwise it is an average city with shopping centers, schools, "church buildings," a central downtown area, a slum, outlying suburbs with endless acres of middle class (three bedroom-two bath, two cars, two t.v.'s and one boat) homes, lots of modern apartments, an upper class side of town, some row houses and a college. Americana!

Now imagine this. You have come here as a tourist to see the city's annual festival. You are a foreigner. Your parents were born and raised in this country but you were born and raised abroad. You do speak English, but with something of an accent. Although you are unaware of it, twelve men you are soon to meet have also come to the city for a brief visit. They are from a nearby town (an ill-reputed town, by the way).

On the opening day of the convention God sends His Spirit. He sends Pentecost! You are part of the onlooking crowd. You hear a man speak, a man named Peter who is one of the twelve men from out of town. And *you* are completely converted to belief in Jesus Christ . . . along with 2,999 other people! You get baptized. The very next day you have a decision to make. Are you going to catch a jet and return home, or will you stay and plunge into the experience of knowing Jesus Christ along with the other 3,119 believers?

Then Peter, a man whom you had never even heard of 24 hours ago, drops a bomb. He doesn't *ask* you anything. He declares! *Everyone* will stay! (Apostles are always going around talking that way.) It is just what your own heart desires. You decide to abandon everything you have known before. You decide to be a true, no-nonsense, no-compromise follower of Jesus Christ. So do the 2,999 other screwballs!

Now for all those little details: where do you sleep? Where do you eat? Soon you find out that about fifty local people who have been converted have made their homes available. Soooo, about sixty of you troop over to each of these typical three-bedroom houses to make yourselves at home. The house you arrive at is packed and running over. You have a bedroll, so you volunteer to sleep in the backyard under the clothesline. Food for all sixty of you will be cooked in that one little family kitchen. But you don't care; no one cares. You all have the Lord.

No moving to the country. No farmhouse. The world around you has not changed a bit. You are right in the middle of modern civilization, pollution, et al.

The next thing you know, the brother who owns the home where you are staying decides to sell it. At first you panic. (There goes the clothesline over your head!) But soon you are truly rejoicing as you see him put up not only his house but also his boat, for sale; then the t.v. sets, including the color console, then the furniture, then the two cars (they don't get very good gas mileage—trade 'em for motorscooters).

Soon you hear that others who are native to the city are also selling everything: homes, cars, week-end cabins, trailers, campers, sailboats, stereos, the works. You want to do the same! You send an overseas telegram and tell your family to sell everything on earth that you own and for them to catch the next supersonic out!

Things are getting pretty wild at this point. It is unimaginable. Everyone has a new perspective: "I *need* so little. If I sell this or this I can give the money to the common fund—more needs of my brothers and sisters will be met. I'm not going to have time or desire to watch t.v. anymore anyway. Golf was just a tranquilizer for my frazzled nerves—I certainly won't need my clubs anymore: I have Jesus Christ!" Really, everyone is selling everything: land, houses, furniture, motorcycles, sewing machines. All security: trust funds, bank accounts, savings, stocks, insurance policies. Everything goes. It is a new life and a new lifestyle in Jesus Christ.

Never again will any of you have anything of this world to trust in. All of you have abandoned your former stations in life. All hopes, all trust in the future, all dreams of security are totally gone. Now your trust is in the Lord and in His church. It has to be; you have nothing else. It will be the Lord or disaster. Christ had better prove to be real and to be faithful, or you are all in a pickle!

The joy of the Lord is out of hand. No one even seems to notice that life has suddenly gone from (the semblance of) security to poverty. Having Jesus Christ is worth it all—and more!

Incidentally, not a whole lot of money to meet the pressing needs of the hour comes in from the sale of all these possessions. Why? Because everyone, being typical twentieth-century human beings, is up to his ears in debt. After paying off the balance due, no one was all that well-to-do after all.

Soon you find yourself looking for a job. Any job. Factory worker, house painter, teacher, cook, anything to help. This is one of the unique features of *true* living in common: *everyone* possible gets a full time job. *Everyone.* And this means routine old city employment, not idyllic country chores. You joyously watch as men and women who were formerly wealthy praise the Lord for the privilege of being hired as waitresses, clerks or computer key punch operators. The jobs they take are hard-working, full time and more-or-less typical. (No one gets a three hour a day job shining shoes so he can just squeak by. . . or so he can spend all his time praying or "serving the Lord full time." No one hatches a get-rich-quick sales organization that will give jobs to all the unemployed brothers. In fact, some of the natural-born promoters and schemers squirm a little bit as they take their first jobs as manual laborers.)

Now that no one owns a home, where will you all live? In solving that dilemma you will get to see the twentieth century way of life blown to smithereens. *Church life always destroys social patterns.* Long held patterns of living, even national heritage and ancient, revered custom, *all* dissolve in the face of an all-consuming church life. Overnight, every social pattern in your life has disappeared. You just lost your entire national heritage! You are going to be relating to all of western civilization in a whole new way. Yes, church life is that revolutionary.

You may think all this is a little too much. If so, then just consider that this is the *only* understanding men had of what it meant to be a follower of Jesus Christ during the first decade of church history.

That image is in dire need of recovery.

There is no good defense for not returning to utter abandonment. The Lord never intended for His followers to have any other image while on this earth. It is a decadent Christianity which allows the present day, wet noodle, Sunday morning, church-going concept to be passed off as the true image of discipleship.

Instinctively, all of you wish to live near one another. This business of being scattered all over the city, living your own scheduled lives behind drawn drapes, is for unbelievers. Forget it! You want to be near the only other 2,999 people in the world who know Jesus Christ. Convention to the wind!

The Apostles comb the town. Is there a place where everyone can live? If not one place, a cluster of places? Sure enough, they find a fraternity house near the campus which is going out of business. About fifty of you pile in there. Next an old hotel is taken over. After that one of the biggest old mansions in town (it has ten bedrooms!) is rented out. Next a new but not yet occupied apartment complex is leased. Finally a block long cul-de-sac is found in a brand new housing tract. It has eight houses on it. This means that one whole street of three bedroom houses will be filled and overflowing with believers.

Suddenly a typical twentieth century three bedroom home located on a nice, quiet, block-long street just isn't typical any more. Each home has about twenty saints living in it. The whole neighborhood resounds with praises and shouts of joy all day long. Instead of a quiet suburban street whose residents are hidden behind their landscaping, the whole cul-de-sac is a beehive of activity. Everybody eats in one or two houses. Everybody meets in another house. "Home" is the whole street.

Just about the same scene is taking place down at the hotel, the campus fraternity and that apartment complex. All are rocking with the praises of God.

Have you ever thought about the three bedroom house, the literal cornerstone of modern civilization? It was invented by pagans for pagans. Today a housing tract of 3,000 houses is planned and built, then 10,000 people come out for the grand opening, buy up the houses and, almost like programmed robots, move in with their matching furniture, draw the drapes, turn on the t.v. set and sit quietly in front of it for the next forty years. You can actually drive through a modern suburb and think it is a ghost town: you hardly ever see a living thing! That is modern (pagan) man. That is not the church.*

What else?

Everyone has given up his own car: some are sold; the rest are pooled. Every morning the saints who have jobs pile into these cars and, accompanied by singing, prayers and praises, set out for work. Those left at home clean the houses, mow the grass, paint; fix up the cars, make repairs, or tear out a wall here and there.

What else?

During the day everyone who can makes sure he gets down to the city park, behind the convention center, to hear the twelve Apostles speak. Then back to the fraternity house, cul-de-sac, hotel or apartment building for more praise and sharing and joy.

---

*It was the same way in Jerusalem. That city was not designed or built for God or His people. It was designed to fit the traditional Hebrew way of life. Then the church came along and upset everything. She didn't use houses as they were designed to be used. The church related to existence on the earth in a whole new way. She didn't care about things other people cared about. The body of Christ forced the very architecture of the city, the way it was planned, laid out and built, the whole system of man's life, to bow to a *new way* of living.

God didn't invent this world's social patterns—patterns which men so obediently yield to generation after generation. God created the church! And the church glorious, just by being what she is, simply rips to pieces all man's social patterns. All of them!

And tomorrow morning it will all start over again!

What you have just read is a twentieth century version of a first century experience. Such a venture would utterly smash the standard, complacent American way of life—or the British, the Australian, the Chinese or any other way of life. You have never seen or experienced anything like what you have just read, but it's out there, waiting to be experienced. It's available to everyone—except those who want security.

God gave this experience to His people for the special purpose of *setting standards* in beginning situations. He also gave it to the church to use in case of economic crises. Furthermore, the Lord intended the church to be so given to Him that living in common, selling all, losing all and breaking all social customs would never seem too much to ask.

It is true that not *all* the early churches practiced living with all goods in common. (The early churches were greatly varied, always defying little categories and neat pigeon holes.) But it is also just as true that living in common was practiced on a far wider scale than most people today realize.*

The Lord longs, just as your own spirit longs, to see a restoration of that overwhelming experience. God began with everyone losing everything. God would begin again in the same way! Today every follower of Jesus Christ should have the right to this experience.

There is much to be said for owning nothing. You have probably wished at some time or other to really see an end to the worldliness in your life. Well, if you have a strong heart, you might just try Jerusalem's approach. It is a sure cure. Jerusalem's technique will de-world you about as quickly and as effectively as it can be done!

*In 160 a.d. (130 years after Pentecost) a bitter pagan antagonist named Lucian referred to the Lord's people as "those imbeciles [who] disdain things terrestrial and hold [them] as belonging to all in common."

In about 190 a.d. a Christian named Tertullian disclosed, "We have all things in common . . . except our wives!"

That means that 160 years after Pentecost the believers were still practicing what was begun in Jerusalem—throughout the *whole* Roman Empire! So it was not a one-shot affair after all. Living in common ought not to be the stepchild that it has become. You ought to have the option of having a go at it—first century style.

You will never be the same again as long as you live. And it will be one of the most glorious, super-spectacular experiences of your life. It will give the Lord ground in your life nothing else can.

Now let us return to the first century and to Jerusalem.

A few days after Pentecost, there was an outbreak of healing. It was suddenly discovered that, in the church, when you had a disease you went to, of all people, an Apostle! This discovery added to the joy and excitement.

This new discovery also set the stage for the next round of growth in the church.

The church has hardly begun, and even though the saints have not yet even recovered from that amazing day of Pentecost, God is about to give them another experience so great that it will almost match Pentecost.

8

The First Four Years

It is exactly three o'clock in the afternoon.

All the shops in the city have closed their doors. It is time for the afternoon sacrifice, and thousands of people are streaming into the temple. Peter and John are in the crowd. Slowly the throng moves up the broad stairways. Just as they reach one of the doorways into the temple, Peter notices some men carrying a lame beggar. As Peter is about to pass him by, he suddenly stops. He is aware of a stirring in his own spirit. For a long moment he stares at the beggar.

Everybody in Jerusalem, including Peter, knew this beggar; he had spent most of his adult life (over twenty years!) sitting right here at this very door. Everyone who had passed through "The Gate Beautiful" knew him on sight.

Peter was a man who had once walked on water, had seen the dead raised, had eaten breakfast with the resurrected Christ! Now he had a stirring in his spirit. Peter had no problem believing that the helpless creature could be healed. The beggar looked up at him; seeing his gaze he expected to receive an offering. Instead, Peter declared, "I have no silver or gold, but I give you what I have." (The financial state of an Apostle, throughout his whole life, ought to be this: flat broke! So it was in the first century.) Suddenly Peter thrust out his hand, grabbed the beggar, and commanded, "In the name of Jesus Christ, the Nazarene, walk!" Half pulled, half struggling on his own, half shocked, half believing, the beggar shot up to his full height!

He was standing!

The poor man stood there a moment gaping in disbelief. But if he could stand, maybe he could walk. So that he tried, too. It worked! He wasted no time. Up and down the steps he walked, crying, shouting, yelling at everyone within hearing distance. (Peter had healed an extrovert!)

Peter and John, surprisingly enough to our century, did not try to capitalize on this spectacular event. The two men walked on into the temple; so did the beggar—only with a lot more noise, shouting and crying. (Very shortly after healing this man the two Apostles slipped out of the temple and back to Solomon's Porch and to their ministry there. They had learned the Lord's way of healing: that it is to be done in *modesty*. Healing should *never* be acclaimed by the healer. Consider *that* in the light of today's practices of healing!)

The beggar, however, was doing a great deal of advertising. After all, he had been lame from birth! Now he was trying out his running skill—in the temple. He was wild with joy. After running, he tried jumping; then he tried leaping. All this time he was broadcasting the amazing news of his healing. Soon almost everyone in the vast afternoon crowd had seen him. As the story was told and retold by the people in the crowd, they started to pour out of the temple and into Solomon's Porch to get a look at these two men who had performed the miracle. (It is likely that by this time the beggar had also made his way to the Porch.) Soon Solomon's Porch was packed with spectators. Peter, wiser because of his experience at Pentecost, wasted no time in proclaiming Christ to the curious throng.

Hundreds immediately believed!

By this time the story of the healing had filtered back to the *temple rulers,* and a small panic had broken out. The first thing they did was to call out the temple guard; they then rounded up the priests and some Sadducees and rushed over to the Porch to arrest the Apostles. But they arrived a little too late to stop a multitude of people from being converted to Christ. How many were converted that afternoon no one knows. But someone estimated that the total number of men in the church had shot up to about 5,000.*

This was the *second* great spurt of growth in the church.

---

*It may be that a total of 5,000 men were converted on that very day. The record is not clear, but it is easy to estimate conservatively that by now there were at least 10,000 people in the church.

The temple administrators could not stop the converts, but they could arrest the Apostles. As a result the two men spent the night in jail. The Apostles had probably had an uneasy feeling that the church was not really welcome in town by the city fathers. Today removed all doubt!

The next morning Peter and John were brought to trial. The court told them, in no uncertain terms, that from that hour on it would be illegal for them to proclaim that Jesus was the Christ. In fact, this came to them in the form of a new city ordinance, passed by the Sanhedrin that very day. The two men were then harrassed, threatened, and released. But just before leaving, they made it very plain to the whole tribunal that they had every intention of breaking this ordinance.

(The believers of the first century were the most law abiding people of the Roman Empire, except in relation to laws that prohibited the preaching of the gospel . . . anywhere! *These* ordinances they broke left and right.)

Just as quickly as it could be done, Peter and John called the church together into one place, and told the whole story of what had happened to them. Instead of responding with sadness or fear, the church burst forth in joy. Then they broke into prayer so awesome that the very earth shook under their feet. The Holy Spirit swept across the gathering. Instantly a new boldness to speak out in the name of Christ struck *all* the *Apostles*. (Note it was not the multitudes but the Apostles who were endowed with this new boldness. The multitudes still did not spearhead—nor hardly even participate in—evangelizing.)

A powerful new wave of proclaiming the gospel hit Jerusalem!

As a result of this new boldness, the church was flooded with yet a *third* influx of converts.

There were so many new converts that the church found itself right back in the situation they had been in just after Pentecost. Once again there was a great housing need; once again there was a great financial need.

It was almost like starting all over again. The church did not even get the luxury of a breathing spell. No one complained, though: it was a glorious problem. Besides, a solution was in the making.

One of the converts, Joseph-Barnabas,* a very wealthy man, owned a great deal of property. Seeing the new need in the church, Barnabas sold everything he had and brought the money to the Apostles. (Most likely he sold his real estate holdings back in his native country of Cyprus). This wonderful act set off a chain reaction; soon everyone in the church had a heart to sell *everything* for Christ to meet this new need. This time the Apostles didn't even have to make the suggestion. People literally didn't care to own anything. Everyone in the church who still had anything of value sold what he had, and the money was brought to the Apostles.

This is the *second* time everyone sold everything. This is madness. And laying it all at the feet of the Apostles! *This* is insane! The sum involved amounted to a vast fortune. (Don't ever do such a thing in the twentieth century. With such a fortune in the hands of men today. . . with today's mentality for buying bigger and better buildings, etc., there is no telling how the money would end up being spent.)

How could any men be so trusted, so trustable? Sure, they were Apostles, but this is still an awesome thing to trust men with. How could the people know those men were *that* trustable? The answer is simple. Their passion was Christ. They had no interest whatsoever in that wealth. Nor did they go out and purchase property with it. (The early church *never* owned property.) They were wise men. They were not empire builders. This was true on the day the money lay at their feet. It would be true all their lives. They were the safest men on earth with such a fortune. Through their entire life-time they never owned anything . . . nor did they ever care to. Find men like that . . . if you can. *They* might be trustable!

At this point, while everyone was giving up all personal ownership of property, a man named Ananias hit on a sure-fire money-making scheme. (He was also about to become a great example of how *not* to make a profit off the church).

*He had picked up the name "Barnabas," which meant "Son of Encouragement," because he was always exhorting and encouraging others.

Everyone who had a job gave his entire salary into the common pool. *Then* everyone in the church had their basic needs met by living in common on the money placed in the pool. Everyone got food and a place to sleep. All other needs were met according to (1) greatest need and (2) funds available. Ananias' plan was simple. He decided to give only *part* of his salary but to *tell* the Apostles he was giving *all*. By doing this he would be able to save back the rest of his monthly income while the church met *all* his needs! In a period of time he could easily save a small fortune.

Ananias put his plan into operation.

He never dreamed what would happen as he came to Peter with the gift and made his statement. Peter's spirit stirred. He saw right into the man's heart. He revealed Ananias' sin and Ananias fell dead on the spot. Later in the day Ananias' wife died in the same manner. The news of their deaths shot through the city. The entire populace was shocked. From that day on everyone in the city, believers and unbelievers, looked upon the Apostles with a very healthy fear. In the meantime God also set a pretty high standard of honesty for those who would ever set out to live in common.

This latest sign, two people dropping dead because they lied to the Holy Spirit, set off a *fourth* great wave of conversions.

The church had begun as 120, then went to 3,000, then to over 5,000 men, and, by this time, who knew how big! (Until this time the numerical size of the church had been estimated as a "multitude," but with this recent growth, a new measurement of size was used. The church was now reckoned as "a *great* multitude." In other words, everyone had lost count!) Solomon's Porch must have been ready to overflow with all the new believers.

(Strangely enough, unbelievers did not venture near Solomon's Porch after that. They seemed to fear these iconoclastic people. Nonetheless, even the unbelievers of the city generally spoke very highly of these followers of Jesus.)

Things in Jerusalem had reached a fever pitch. The whole city was rocked by these people. Every day more and more people were converted. To top it off a *second* wave of healing set in. Great numbers of people were again recovering from disease. Hundreds were healed at the hands of the Apostles.

This season of healing set off the *fifth* great influx of converts.

It happened this way: news of people being healed in Jerusalem reached the ears of people living in all the nearby towns. Soon people from those cities began flocking into Jerusalem, bringing their sick to be healed by the twelve.

Perhaps the people in the other towns were getting jealous. Perhaps they were saying, "If those Apostles are just going to stay in one city, I'm not going to miss the joy of knowing Christ. If the church will not come to me, I'll go to it."

Five great waves of growth! One right after the other! The church was swept with an atomosphere of joy, awe and expectancy. It was quite a place to be!

Church life is always exciting.

The body of believers grew larger still as out-of-towners got healed and saved and then decided to *stay* in Jerusalem to be part of the church! The church was so large by this time that the term "multitude," and even the term "great multitude," was outdated. Now the church was reckoned simply as *"multitudes."* They had not only lost count, they had lost comprehension of their size.

This brings us to a fascinating question: how did the early church grow? What *method* did the church employ in order to grow? What was its "evangelistic program"?

It had none!

The Jerusalem church reached its great size by four means: (1) incredible events, such as Pentecost; (2) seasons of healing which usually followed such events; (3) the Apostles' daily ministry at Solomon's Porch; and, finally (4) the gatherings in the homes which drew many people to Christ.

Please notice that such things as "soul winning" and "evangelistic meetings" have not been introduced in the history of the church. These things came into being many years later (1,800 years later!) The whole spiraling growth of the church in Jerusalem had an unplanned, spontaneous flavor about it.

The church is now about four years old.

Please notice that *still* absolutely *no one* in the church is evangelizing or doing anything, *except* the Apostles. Also notice that the church has no gifted men, no special offices, no structure, no organization. Just twelve Apostles and over 10,000 people!

Everything has been like a dream in Jerusalem. The only real problem the church has ever had was a little tiff with the local administrators. Such good fortune is about to end. Serious trouble awaits the church just ahead.

It is about 34 a.d.

9

The First Trouble

The twelve Apostles have been arrested. They are in jail awaiting trial. There is a good chance they will all be put to death.

The case will be tried by the Sanhedrin. (The Sanhedrin is in charge of only the religious affairs of the city but is the closest thing to a Jewish government during this age of enemy occupation.) The seventy men of the Sanhedrin have been watching their city being turned upside down over the man, Jesus Christ. Finally, today, they have been forced to take action to restore religious order to Jerusalem. It will probably be necessary for them to put the twelve to death, just as they had the Lord five years earlier.

Why such extreme measures? Why did they want to kill twelve men? Was it *really* religious devotion? No! It was the way things were going: if they did not stop the Apostles, it was highly possible the whole city might one day turn to follow Christ. Where would that leave the Sanhedrin? It would leave them without power or position. They would be out of a *job*.

That was what had them worried.

The religious system had good reason to be threatened by this new movement led by these twelve men. The twelve had repeatedly broken the city ordinance which absolutely prohibited proclaiming the gospel of the resurrected Christ and, along with it, this infuriating Gospel of the Kingdom they proclaimed. The ordinance had done no good. The twelve got bolder than ever after the ordinance was passed. Furthermore, this new thing called "the church" was growing by leaps and bounds. Even people from Judea had recently begun to pour into Jerusalem bringing their sick to be healed.

Now Jerusalem was choked full of these out-of-towners; some of them were even staying and becoming part of the church! The whole thing was getting out of hand. The time had come to put a stop to the twelve and to the church.

The situation in Jerusalem at this time was a story as old as fallen man. Something new had come along which was a threat to the existence of the establishment. The "new" had to be stopped by, and for the sake of, the "established."

Watch the religious system—*any religious system*—when this point is reached: some kind of persecution is bound to start.

The twelve Apostles were led into the Hall of Polished Stones for questioning by the council. Their answers certainly did nothing to calm the fears of their interrogators. Never had any defendants spoken so boldly or with such authority as these men. The charge against them, proclaiming that Jesus was the Messiah, could invoke the death sentence, but they did not have even a trace of fear. All twelve men stood right there before their judges and flatly stated that they had no intention of being quiet about Jesus the Christ.

This august council had every reason to believe what they were being told, too.

Why? Something had happened yesterday to prove, beyond any doubt, that these men meant what they were saying. Yesterday the Sanhedrin had put the Apostles in prison; last night they had "broken jail" . . . . assisted by an angel, no less! Instead of fleeing the city, as any sane men would have done, they marched directly out of the jail, back up to the *temple,* and there started proclaiming the Gospel of Jesus Christ *all over again!* Later the local law enforcement officers told the Sanhedrin about the jail break, and then—sheepishly—told where they had found the twelve men *this* morning. And now, here they stood, facing possible death, and they were still declaring that if they got out alive they would go right back and break the law again!

In the face of such open defiance of law and order, the Sanhedrin was almost honor-bound to pass the death sentence. They probably *would* have, except for the words of one revered elder statesman among them. His name was Gamaliel, and whenever he spoke, his advice was always carefully considered. He requested that the court recess for a private session. In that closed meeting Gamaliel pointed out that there was a good chance this new movement might simply collapse. . . if given time.

Gamaliel's words saved the lives of the twelve. Instead of sentencing them to death, the Sanhedrin decided to assign each of the men to a brutal beating . . . . the dreaded thirty-nine lashes.

So it was that each Apostle tasted his very first suffering for Christ! After they had all been hauled out and beaten, the twelve were ushered back before the Sanhedrin. But even this horrible experience of the lash had not squelched their boldness. They were bloody, half dead, and groggy, but they were *still* defiant. With nothing else they could do, the religious leaders threatened the men and set them free. At best the Sanhedrin had ended up with a draw.

This was the first serious persecution to come to the followers of Christ. What was their reaction?

Gloom?

The twelve men were absolutely overflowing with joy as they left the courtroom. They had finally been counted worthy to suffer for their Lord!

They were exhilarated.

The imprisonment, the break-out, the threatened death sentence, the beatings, the demand that they speak no more of Christ, all this caused the twelve to march right back into the Porch, into the homes, and speak out more boldly than ever. Once more (for the *sixth* time) the size of the church shot upward, this time under the impelling blaze of twelve burning men.

Naturally, the meeting in the Porch increased in size. The number of the houses where the church met also increased. (Probably well over 200 homes were being used for church gatherings by now.) It was a truly amazing hour.

The most conservative guess as to the size of the church by this time would put it above 15,000 believers. In fact 20,000 would be far more realistic.

While all these exciting things were happening, time has

been passing. The church is five years old.

The first serious trouble the church has ever known is behind them. The first persecution came from the *outside,* that is, from the *religious* world. Just ahead is a second round of trouble, but this time it will come from *inside* the church itself.

It is about 35 a.d.

10

Seven Men

Twenty thousand people.

Think of all the problems.

Living in common.

Think of all the details.

Only twelve Apostles to attend to everything.

Little things were always wrong.

Something big was bound to go wrong one day.

And it did!

Imagine what 20,000 people living in common would mean! For instance, food had to be found and bought every day. Then, some way, it had to be distributed to feed 20,000 mouths. All this buying and distributing was the job of the Apostles—plus a myriad other responsibilities. Of course ministry came first. So, everything they did to oversee living in common they did in their spare time. For other things there were other people who helped. But "help" amounted to anybody who happened to be standing nearby when the problem arose.

The Apostles never did get "organized." The whole thing of the church living in common, and all other matters, were cared for on a grand scale of chaos. All help was volunteer and catch-as-you-can. Now, volunteer labor in the Lord's house is precious, always offered out of a heart of love and a real desire to help. Nonetheless, it can be very undependable at times.

But that was all right. No one complained—at least not loudly. After all, even the Apostles still had clear memories of how sloppy, undependable and thick-headed they had been . . . and not so long ago, either!

So the church in Jerusalem was as it should be: sloppy, chaotic, without organization, structureless, unplanned, with every new need being met by volunteer labor. It was all cock-eyed and whacky and everyone loved it that way.

For instance, someone would volunteer to do a certain job. Great! He'd run into a few obstacles and put some details off for a while. A few months later he had forgotten all about the job, left it, and never told a soul he had quit. Suddenly *everything* was going wrong. Everyone got frustrated. Maybe even a bit tiffed. Then everyone started picking up the pieces and the whole process started over again. Some dear brother, observing all this confusion... caused by that other very undependable brother, figured he could do the job better. So he'd take over the job. A few more months would pass; and the second brother has everything and everybody fouled up! Sure enough, he is just as undependable as the last fellow! The whole thing falls apart again. Over and over, year after year, it was the same story. Everyone got exposed, no one was so great after all. Everyone learned a lesson.

The whole business of church life is always a seed bed for humility.

The church has now existed for about seven years without ever getting organized... or structured. It is all stuck together by love and forebearance. It is a mess; it's like a big lump of goo that just sort of oozes along.

So it was bound to happen.

Things *finally* got out of hand. Maybe it was the sheer size of it all. Maybe it was because seven years had passed. Or maybe it was because the Lord knew it was finally time to begin... just *barely* begin... to raise up some more men of God. Anyway, the church had its first big problem in about the seventh year of church history.

It happened this way.

Some of the widows who were not originally from Jerusalem, began looking at the amount of food they got, then looking over at the size of the food rationings of some of the local widows and then making some comparisons. They didn't like what they saw.

Probably some overly zealous young single brother from Jerusalem—unconsciously—let his local prejudices show as he doled out the daily rations.

Anyway, the Greek-speaking widows started murmuring. The murmuring spread. It soon infected the whole church. And like those following Moses in the wilderness, once the murmuring broke out, the spiraling blessing of God leveled off . . . then stopped.

Murmuring always stops the forward move of God.

The amazing thing is *not* that murmuring had broken out in the church of God. The *amazing thing* is the church actually went seven *long* years before such a thing happened! (That is probably *still* the world's record for unflawed unity among God's people!) People, then and now, can be so naive. They actually believe that all those dear, sweet people they have been thrown together with would just never start a church spat.

The fact is, it will always happen. (There are *no* exceptions!!)

Praise the Lord that when the *first* internal problem in church history happened, *the Apostles* were there to handle it. Once again we are brought back to that key thing of Apostleship. It is *Apostles* who raise up churches. No Apostle, no church life. Without them this whole enterprise called "church" is doomed before it is ever begun.

You may feel you would really like to experience church life just the way first century believers did. You may feel this is what you want and what you need. You may feel that it is central in God's purpose. You may even feel you are ready to give your life for such a thing. But your chances of getting together with a group of people and ending up with true church life are slim indeed . . . unless you *begin* with Apostleship. It is at times like these—times when strife breaks out—times which *must* come—that the necessity of Apostleship is clearly seen. *Apostleship precedes church life.*

(Today there is a strong feeling among many believers that the practice of the church can begin *spontaneously:* that a group of people needs no special help, that "God can raise up a church that has true *body life.* He does not need Apostles to help him. All we need to do is have a group of people who love one another, meet in homes, obey the Scripture, etc., and soon we will have the church as it should be." Yes, you are right, such a group might really *begin* spontaneously, and might get along very well with no one to help them . . . in the beginning. The fellowship of that

73

group may really be neat. It may even have a little of the true flavor of church life, but you can be sure of this: *your little group cannot survive long.* For one thing, God will *never* allow a so-called "spontaneous" church. Not even when such groups appear to be popping up everywhere, all over the earth . . . spontaneously! Odd as it may seem, the spontaneous church is contrary to God's ordained way. Hundreds upon hundreds of "home groups" spring up every year—mostly among very dear and very consecrated young people. They try to have "body life," to be a spontaneous church, and they have invariably fallen apart. Such groups have proven over and over again that such a thing is just not possible! Yet there is always *another* group coming along to take the place of the last one. This one feels absolutely certain that *they* will make it; they will be that one exception where all others have failed. Then mark this: in *all* the first century there is *no* record of a "spontaneous" church. There was always *outside* help!! And add this: if there had been no Apostles in those all-important formative years, you can be sure *even* the *Jerusalem* church would have collapsed! To properly survive you *must* have outside help of Apostolic stature. Now, just try to find *that* kind of help! When you finally come to the point that you insist on *that* standard—Apostle-size help—you really face a problem! If you settle for less you will only end up with a broken heart! And be careful if you think you have found such help! There are a lot of people around very willing to help you. Some look pretty neat. They have "seen the church!" But they have *not* had years of experiencing the church.

What *are* your chances of finding help of the stature God had in the first century? Consider this. There were about twenty to twenty-five men during all the first century who wore the title "Apostle." Even a number that small was a bumper crop compared to *any* century since then! So trying to find men of Apostolic stature to help your little group may turn out to be a bigger, much, much bigger problem than you think. In the process of looking for them you may even discover why true church life has been virtually nonexistent for the last 1,700 years!)

The murmuring eventually reached the ears of the Apostles. They immediately went into a huddle to figure out what to do with this first church spat. We gain real insight into these twelve men as we see their decision. They acted so practically. Nothing spiritual in their decision at all. And nothing legalistic. (They didn't conjure up a couple dozen rules and slap them on everyone to obey. Rules *do* always stop murmuring.)* The decision was simple. The crowds were too big for the Apostles alone to handle the food rationing. Conclusion: someone else should do it!

That was the simple solution! The twelve hammered out the details of how to do this and then called the church together.

(Please notice the scope of the Apostles' responsibility at this point in church history. They were totally in charge of *all* ministry and *all* administration! The only thing they were *not* in charge of was those *home meetings!* If a church is *young,* and if Apostles are present, those Apostles will be in charge of almost everything. But you can also be sure that if he is a *true* Apostle the day will come when he turns the church administration over to others. Furthermore, he himself will eventually completely leave the church, that is, he will actually leave town. And the home meetings will always be totally free, whether he is present or not.)

On the day the church came together, "all in one place," to hear the Apostles' decision, it was probably to experience the first "church business meeting" in history. The Apostles asked the church to pick out *seven* men to handle the distribution of the rations. The twelve then set out some guidelines by which the church should pick these men.

Here are those guidelines.

First, these seven men must be men who have been around long enough to have been well observed and well tested. That is, have they held a steady job? Are they dependable and honest? Not lazy, not poor at following instructions? In other words these seven men should all have obtained a *good report* from others in the church. *Secondly,* these men should be full of the Holy Spirit. *Thirdly,* they should be wise, practical men. It was a practical-minded job.

As soon as the Apostles finished explaining all this, the

---

*Notice the Apostles did not solve the problem by the time-honored approach of attacking those doing the murmuring or those doing the short changing. No! And they didn't excommunicate a raft of people. They just worked out the problem.

multitude responded excitedly. Right then and there the church went to work selecting the seven. How did 20,000 people select seven people? We do not know. (Certainly not by committee!)

Soon it was done. Another meeting was called. This time it was the Apostles who were awaiting the surprise. One by one, the seven men were brought up to stand before the Apostles. (Two of the seven men who came forward we will meet again in later chapters. One is a man named Stephen, the other a man named Phillip.)

The Apostles watched. It must have been quite a scene. When all seven men were standing before them, it was the Apostles' turn again. The twelve did something that day never done before in *all church* history. (Of course, church history was only about seven years old!)

The Apostles *laid hands* on the seven.

The business of the laying on of hands has a multitude of meanings. That day it probably meant the Apostles were passing on some of their own divinely appointed responsibility to the seven. It was also a sign that on this day the *body* of Christ was passing on to seven specific parts of that body, some special functions to perform for the whole body.

And *that* brings up a fascinating question. Just *what were "the seven?"*

Were they deacons?

No!

Were they elders?

No!

Apostles, maybe?

No!

Then what were they?

The answer is so simple: they were *the seven*. No more. No less.

If you had been there that day and walked up to one of the Apostles after the meeting and said; "Peter, are these men *elders* or are they deacons?" Peter would have looked at you blank faced and responded, "What's an elder? What do you mean by deacon?" The Apostles had never dreamed of such an idea. *Not at that point in time.*

Or if you had asked Peter what the duties or the qualifications of an elder were, he would have been just as dumbfounded. Furthermore, if you had asked him for a good, clear definition of what an *Apostle* was, and what the duties of an Apostle were, he would have had to answer, "I don't have the faintest idea . . . all I know is that I am one! Watch me and find out!"

The point is this: even though the church was about seven years old, no one had ever dreamed of *elders.* The idea of "elders" in this new enterprise called "church" had never been heard of.

The same was true of deacons. A deacon as something *special* was also *un*heard of. All believers were *deacons* . . . for the word simply meant *servant* . . . a very, very common word in use in that day. All believers considered themselves *servants* of Christ.

It may be hard for you to realize at first, but the Apostles had never even conceived of the idea that some day offices such as "overseer" would exist. They never dreamed men would one day come along and exhibit a gift which would cause those men to be called "evangelist!" They never dreamed of the church having *evangelists,* nor of men with a gift which would cause them to be designated *'prophet."*

Yes, such a day would come. The church would have such men. But that day was still way out in the future!! Right now, seven years after Pentecost, there were still only two groups in the church: *Apostles* and 20,000 believers (seven of those 20,000 had the job of rationing food!) Elders, prophets, teachers, evangelists, etc., are still un-dreamed of.

In our own century this simple fact is completely lost. Today men pour over first century literature trying their best to figure out: "What is an elder? What does he do?" or "What is a prophet? What does a prophet do?"

Stopping there might not be so dangerous. But to go on and say: "Now here are the duties of an elder. You take this list; memorize all the duties of an elder; then go do those things." That is bad enough, but men do not stop there *either.* They start inspecting one another. "Maybe *he* is a prophet!" "If *you* are an evangelist, then you are supposed to do this and this and this!"

Pitiful!

But an even *worse* tragedy comes when believers of our age begin meeting, for example, to have a "New Testament church." First they meet in homes, and they meet with the hope and expectation of having true church life; invariably the idea comes up that the group needs elders. (They don't.) They also are full of high hopes that the Lord will very soon, and quite spontaneously, raise up evangelists, prophets, etc.—maybe in just a very *few months,* too! (He won't.) That is simply impossible. As you will see, it took *twelve* years for such a thing to happen in Jerusalem . . . and it happened only after men went through years of experience and fiery trials. And they also had twelve Apostles to nudge things along. It won't take *less* time today for true eldership to emerge, especially when the level of church life is so far from any first century experience. It will take a long, long time for any men today to see *the church* raise up and organically produce such things as elders, prophets, etc. The situation in Christendom today is so far behind in the ingredients necessary to properly produce true elders, etc., that we are every bit as much at the starting gate as Jerusalem was.

The point is this: church life first produces the man; the *man creates the office;* the office does not create the man. As the story of the early church unfolds, you will see the Holy Spirit, and the Holy Spirit alone, raise men up and give them functions and offices and gifts. At first, though, those men did not know they had some gift or office given them by the Holy Spirit. They unconsciously began to carry out their gifts and their offices. At first the things they *did,* and the things they *were,* went unlabeled, unsung, unhonored and *almost* unnoticed. Then, a few months or years after these men entered into their function, the Apostles began to scratch their heads; something unusual was going on! Finally, they figured out that the Holy Spirit had done something *new.* HE had given gifts—gifted men—to the church. HE had given offices to the church. The Apostles realized that God planned to give more offices to the church than just Apostleship. Probably they were amazed at the discovery.

And how did the Apostles finally figure this out? *Not* by reading a text book.

Then how?

By observing the men who had been given the offices! By actually seeing the gifts! By seeing the men *function* with those gifts. They figured it out by looking at the men who were walking around in front of them.

It was only at that point, after these gifted men had spent *years* in the experience of church life, long *after* the Holy Spirit had planted the gift in the man and let that gift gradually grow to full stature, long after his gift was in full operation, that the Apostles figured out God had sent gifts and offices to the church. When that point was reached, the Apostles started trying to figure out what label to pin on these men. The label—the name—was there only as a means to describe what those men *already* were. The title sought to proclaim what they had already been doing . . . organically. The name by which they were called only described what the Holy Spirit had already done in them!

Certainly the Apostles did not make up a list and hand it to those men and say, "Now here's what an elder is, do this. Here's what an evangelist is, so you do this and this." No, to figure out what an elder was they *watched* those men whom the Holy Spirit had made elders. The list came from watching the men themselves.

Once more: all this, as you will see, took *twelve* years . . . with the help of twelve Apostles . . . don't forget!

Where does that leave us? At the starting gate, that's where!

What must be done in our own age to get back to these first principles? The answer is clear!

The first step is to drop our fly-by-night mentality. To see what a real elder or a real evangelist is, we must first see a full restoration of true church life. That must be the *first* order of business. You must not rush the "gifts" part! If you do you will *never* have church life! Years must pass. The Holy Spirit must have time to do His work. Furthermore, the church must probably pass through a number of hair-raising crises! It is then that true eldership begins coming into focus.

79

Then the Holy Spirit will raise up elders, and evangelists, etc., through the church. At that point everybody can stand back and say, "Oh, so that is what an elder is; so that is what an evangelist is!"

What is an evangelist anyway?

Who knows?? Only by seeing church life restored do we find out!

In other words, the Holy Spirit is just as capable *today* of raising up such men, such offices, such functions, as He was in the day of the early church. Elders, prophets and evangelists are all in there, *inside* the Holy Spirit. It is part of the innate nature of the Holy Spirit to raise up elders, prophets, evangelists, etc. They are *literally* part of His nature. But the Holy Spirit needs two things, the same two things He needed in the first century. He needs *true church experience* and He needs *time.*

True prophets, evangelists and other gifted men are all products of a locatable church life—not seminaries, not personal talents, not individual preferences. Throughout all the first century it was the Holy Spirit in practical church life who raised up men. Tragically we have been devoid of such an "incubator" in our day.

Then what is the real significance of the seven men the church has just chosen if they are not elders, deacons, evangelists or teachers? These men are just the first small hint that such gifts, such offices, such men, might exist out there in the future somewhere. Things like elders and deacons are still years away!

Anyway, the church selected the seven, the Apostles laid hands on them, the seven went to work on the food problem, and the murmuring ended! The church was back on course.

Once more—just as soon as the murmuring ended—the church had a population explosion! Once more, for the *seventh* time to be exact, people were being saved; the church was growing by leaps and bounds.

We can be safe in assuming that the total number of people had reached 20,000 by now!

During this seventh spurt of growth something *new* happened. As always, many people were being saved, but this time even *temple priests* were getting converted! This marked a turning point in the church—it was unprecedented. In fact the conversion of priests caused an *immediate* impact on church history.

What was that impact?

The news that priests were being converted to Christ started a panic in Jerusalem's religious system. The Sanhedrin hit the dome.

The religious system can always handle a new movement, just as long as it reaches only the man on the street. But when this new work takes away men *inside* the structure itself, then things happen. An attack is on its way.

(At that moment the church was rejoicing to see professional religionists converted to Christ; but many years from now these believing priests will greatly damage the Jerusalem church. But that is another story.)

As word reached the Sanhedrin that priests were now believing in Christ, they immediately started drawing up plans to destroy the church.

By the way, this gives you one more clue into the "office" of *the seven: their jobs did not last long!* You see, as a result of persecution that is about to begin, those seven men held their jobs for only a very brief period of time. One of the seven will soon be killed, the other six will flee the city. Their job probably did not last for over a year. So you can see conclusively that these men were not deacons, as often supposed. They were simply "the seven."

The church is headed for a mammoth upheaval. Persecution of the first magnitude is about to fall on the Jerusalem church. This will turn out to be one of the darkest hours in all church history.

Let us see what set off this holocaust.

Tiberius has just ended his twenty-three year reign as Emperor of the Roman Empire. Gaius Caligula has just been named the new Emperor in his place. And you are about to meet two young men who are remembered better than both these emperors put together.

It is 37 a.d.

11

Titans Two

Two of the most outstanding men of the first century are about to clash head-on. The fury of that clash will bring the church very close to annihilation.

We need to take a look at these two men for they greatly affect the history of the Jerusalem church.

The first of the two young men is Stephen—one of the seven.

The second is a young man named Saul, an unbeliever. Let us look first at Stephen.

If Stephen was twenty-five when he was converted, then today he is approximately thirty-three. Only recently have we heard from him for, until now, he has been going through his "wasted years." At last, he has emerged.

It is interesting to note that most men in the early church did not become true vessels *sent out* by God until their mid-thirties or early forties! All the well known men of the first century went through a prolonged period of preparation, a time of doing nothing. Stephen was undeniably one of the greatest figures of the early church. He was the *first* great figure to emerge after the Apostles. He was their equal in every way. Stephen, in fact, has few peers in all church history. Nonetheless, even he went through a long period of total inactivity and of being nothing.

What produced Stephen? That is an exciting question!

In Jerusalem Stephen was a foreigner. He was a Jew, yes, but in the Holy City a foreigner nonetheless. He was originally from outside Judea, and, unlike Judean Jews, grew up amidst the culture of the Greeks and Romans. It was a trip to Jerusalem which first brought Stephen to Christ . . . and to the church. He doubtlessly heard Peter speak on the day of Pentecost and was converted to Christ. Stephen was nothing but a face in the crowd that day, but he fell in love with his new Lord. That love initiated the great transformation which took place in Stephen during the following eight years.

What were the ingredients of his transformation?

The first ingredient was added on the day he got saved. He was *baptized* . . . along with about 2,999 other people! (Please note that he did not speak in tongues, nor was he empowered from on high, nor did he go out preaching the gospel. None of the 3,000 did.)

In the days immediately following, Stephen had his second big experience. He decided to give up everything—country, friends, family, home and job to stay in Jerusalem. He *sold all* and *gave all:* he became penniless. This was his introduction to a *state of utter abandonment* and for him it was a "for-the-rest-of-my-life" decision. He would walk the earth the way his Lord walked it, owning absolutely nothing.

Thirdly, Stephen threw himself wholly into the life and fellowship of the *church.*

To put it in a word, Stephen obeyed the Gospel of the Kingdom. He began with absolutely *nothing;* he gave all his time, his whole life, just to experience the depths of his Lord.

This all happened on the first two days of his new life!

The fourth big thing in Stephen's life happened when he moved into a house with dozens of other believers and called it "home." All he had was about three feet by six feet on someone's living room floor! In his new home he began the glorious adventure of something called *corporate living.* (There is nothing like it.) It was Stephen's unique privilege to live through those glorious, hectic, unforgettable, outrageous days of the beginning of the church. Under those crowded, ever-changing conditions, Stephen learned to experience his Lord *with others.* This served to keep him human while he was learning to be divine! So add corporate living as an ingredient in Stephen's life. Put another way, he had the neatest experience God ever invented to expose men for what they really are—yet grow them up in Christ.

What came next? Stephen went to the temple area every day and sat at the feet of the Apostles. With thousands of others, he heard the Apostles' instruction and thrilled to discover his riches in Christ. He heard things of the depths of Christ. He was introduced to practical ways of experiencing and knowing Christ. He was pointed to the depths of the riches of Christ. The Apostles made Christ very real, very practical, very available.

We might add another thing he learned from the Apostles. He began learning a little about submission and authority. He learned submission to authority . . . and he watched the men who held that authority exercise it with humility and meekness. So, add to Stephen's life the experience of being under the authority and teaching of an Apostle.

Leaving the Porch every evening, six days a week, he went back to his crowded home and met together with his brothers and sisters. There he tasted again the corporate experience of pursuing Christ; there he also drank of the joy of home meetings. Little by little Stephen was learning to experience Christ individually and corporately. Stephen was becoming *rich* in the experience of Christ.

Stephen also did one other thing in those days: he made a lot of mistakes.

Sometimes he got discouraged; perhaps he even had some serious problems adjusting to his peculiar roommates! It was probably in the daily things that he learned his first lessons in being exposed, in brokenness, confession, forgiving, adjusting, being forgiven, submitting, mutual forebearance, and maybe even the embarrassment of being submitted to! And when even *newer* converts than he came moving in, he learned patience, tenderness, gentleness, compassion, understanding, and encouragment. Stephen learned humanity and humility.

At times Stephen, like any new believer, just *knew* he would never make it. But he always had something very special going for him during those dark days: he had his brothers and sisters to encourage him, to hold him up, and to carry him on. That was part of the beauty and one of the biggest secrets of the early church.

In the church you make it because the quest is corporate.

One last thing. He was a young man and yet he did *not* serve the Lord. That was an awesome advantage. Why did he never go out on "preaching missions?" Why did he *waste* his twenties and early thirties? Why didn't the Apostles put him to work? Maybe it was because the Apostles recalled that in the nearly four years they lived with Jesus they spent only fourteen days in actual service!

Perhaps the greatest single tragedy of present day Christianity is found here: the habit of putting zealous young men into full time service for Christ. It is without first century parallel. It wrecks men's lives. (How could anyone in his twenties have possibly come to *know* the depths of Jesus Christ?) Eventually, somewhere, someday it wrecks men's lives.

There are no exceptions.

Stephen got to sit. Thanks be unto God.

So here is what the young convert, Stephen, had going for him: (1) the words of the Apostles *and* the experience of living under authority; (2) the meetings in homes; (3) his corporate experience of Christ and his exposure among his brothers and sisters; and most of all, (4) the growing ability to experience the presence of Christ throughout the day . . . without being wrecked by something called "full time service in the Lord's work."

Little by little he began to know and to live by the Christ who dwelt within him. Little by little Christ grew in Stephen. Day after day the Lord wove His divine nature into this once ordinary man. The new convert was slowly being transformed into full stature. As the years went by Stephen began knowing truly deep experiences with Christ.

You might think this all very beautiful but do you realize that *by twentieth century standards* Stephen was a backslider! He never witnessed, never worked any miracles, had *not* "gone out all over the world preaching the gospel"—and yet he had witnessed the day of Pentecost! He had the "Pentecost experience" on the very day it happened. Now everyone knows that if you have the experience of Pentecost you are endowed with power from on high. And after that you are supposed to go out and turn the world upside down.

Well, Stephen *did not.* He was there the day it happened and for the next eight years he didn't do anything or go anywhere. There is no record that he, the 3,000 or anyone else, *except the twelve,* did any soul-winning, worked any miracles, or preached any messages. Even the Apostles didn't leave the city limits. So, by our present day concept of Pentecost, even the Apostles were disobedient!! Let the record show, none of those 3,000 who went through Pentecost did *anything* for eight years. By the present day concept of Pentecost, everyone who actually experienced Pentecost was a backslidden, disobedient disciple!

Today's concept of the experience of Pentecost goes further: "After you have had the experience of Pentecost you will be endued with power, (healing, evangelism, etc.) *and* you will have the key to the victorious life and will overcome *all* spiritual problems. You will be prosperous and happy. You will be like the 3,000 on the day of Pentecost. Take the short cut. Turn the world upside down. Experience Pentecost."

But that is *not* the first century version of Pentecost! *Only* the twelve were empowered at Pentecost. Not even the 120 got in on that.

The twelve were empowered only because they received the Holy Spirit *and* had just graduated from nearly four years of preparation under the tutorship of Jesus Christ. God felt that *only* those twelve men were fit vessels, *trustable vessels,* to handle power! They, and they alone, graduated that day. God has never shown any interest in empowering *new converts,* or in sending out new converts, or in giving His power to improperly prepared men! Furthermore, *no one* went out preaching the gospel . . . not even the Apostles! But most of all—and this fact smashes the whole twentieth century idea of the "power of Pentecost"—absolutely no one besides the 12 showed any sign of having power with God for the next eight years after Pentecost! Not one person in all the 3,108 who actually went through Pentecost gave even one sign of being "empowered." None! And that situation lasted for eight years after Pentecost! And how many of the 3,108 showed signs of being empowered at the end of eight years . . . 3,000? 1,000? 120? No! Not even twelve. How many then? One . . . one lone man, and only *one.*

Men all over the earth today are saying "what we need is

the experience of Pentecost!" Absolutely right! But what was the Pentecost experience for 3,108 people? Was it going out? No! Was it empowerment? No! Was it a myriad of independent ministries flowering overnight? No! The true Pentecost experience was a sitting down experience, not a going out experience. The results of Pentecost were this: 3,000 people sat down for eight years and did nothing; they sat under Apostles; they were in a practical, visible, attendable church. This was the true result of Pentecost. Yes, we need the experience of Pentecost today . . . desperately. Men need to sit down in church life and do nothing for eight years. *This* was the true manifestation of Pentecost . . . first century style.

Unthinkable?? Does eight years seem like a long time to you? It was not at all in that day. In fact, by first century standards Stephen set a speed record. He was one of the very few men in all the history of the early church whose preparation period was *less* than ten years! So we are all forced to admit that something is amiss here somewhere! Either the early church or present day Christianity is *way* off course! Which?

Watch and see; the story of the early church will make that answer so clear.

As you have noticed, there have always been *only* two groups of believers in the Jerusalem church: the Apostles and the multitude. Many people were probably wondering if God would ever raise up anyone besides the Apostles. Then, suddenly, Stephen broke out of the ranks. He performed miracles and proclaimed the gospel with power. Overnight there were no longer *two* groups in the church (Apostles and believers). There were now three "groups:" Apostles, the multitudes and *Stephen!*

It has taken nearly a decade, but *at last* it has happened. True, only *one* man—*but what a man.* And he has grown up organically, naturally! No formalized training produced Stephen. The inward work of the Holy Spirit and the daily experience of life in the church produced this awesome vessel.

When this very new, spectacular event occurred, what was everyone's reaction? Were they surprised it was Stephen? Did they really believe he was genuine? Had they not seen him depressed, weeping, even defeated? Had they not seen him in moments of great weakness, even in defeat? How could *he*, ordinary Stephen, have become such a spiritual man? He had been under incredibly close scrutiny for nearly a decade. Every fault in his character was common knowledge.

Yes, the church had confidence in Stephen, and it was *because* of how well they knew him, *because* of the things they had seen him go through. They had watched him grow up in Christ. Through all his trials, they had seen him turn again and again to the Lord. After *years* of pressure, testing and exposure, he had come forth as a proven vessel. His spirit, his love for Christ, had been proven by years of practical, daily, bedrock experience, all of which went on right out in the open—in the church of God.

This is how it was throughout that whole century. The servants of the Lord were trusted because they had been exposed and broken . . . in full view of everyone. In our day, because there is no church life to do all this exposing, men have not allowed themselves to be known. Unfortunately today the whole relgious system is set up in such a way that it shields men from exposure and cushions the breaking the Lord wants to do to prepare vessels. Men today have simply not lived in the open glare of the church. They have never discovered the wretchedness of their own souls.

This is a source of great loss.

When Stephen proclaimed the Gospel, everyone knew his words were honest, his power real, his humility a fact. Furthermore he could never have gotten away with a "holy glow" or "gothic steepled prayers." He would not have dared to pretend in front of a group of people who knew him like a book. In the church everybody knows you! No, Stephen was not some sharp, gifted speaker from out of town . . . with a half dozen knock 'em dead sermons . . . whose private, spiritual life was totally unknown to the church. Stephen's devotion to his Lord was a solidly established fact! Established before the eyes of thousands of his brothers and sisters.

A life proven in the fire of church life! That is the test every man who ministers the Gospel should *have* to experience.

So a young man named Stephen, one of the seven, a man full of the Holy Spirit, had broken out of the ranks and was matching the power, matching the authority and matching the ability of the Apostles!

See what that means.

Until now only twelve men of great spiritual responsibility had ever been raised up. They had been raised up under the tutorage of Jesus Christ Himself. Jesus Christ was the *only* person who had been able to raise up men of Apostolic stature. It even took the Lord nearly four years to raise up Apostles, and He worked at it eighteen hours per day. And He was God! But now something *new* and exciting had happened. Jesus Christ, of course, had ascended; He was no longer there! He was not on earth, physically, as He was with the twelve! Nonetheless, even in the Lord's absence a man of Apostolic stature had been produced!

That is historical!

So it was not the physical Christ, walking about Galilee, who had raised up Stephen: it was Christ in the church.

What Christ once did, the *church* was now doing!

You might say that Christ inside Stephen had done in eight years what the Christ living with twelve men had done in four years. The physical Christ, the Christ who raised up the twelve Apostles, was no longer on the earth; but, praise God, the indwelling Spirit and the church had come to make up the difference!

Praise God, the church had come!

Now hear this.

Restore the *life* of the church, restore the true, real, vital experience of church life; add to that the experience of knowing the indwelling of Christ *the way Stephen knew Him,* allow men to experience what Stephen experienced, go through what Stephen went through, and *then* you will start seeing men of his stature upon this earth again!

Anyway, Stephen was the first man beyond the Apostles to show evidence of being endued with power by the Holy Spirit. That bears repeating. Eight years after Pentecost there were thirteen men on this earth who showed evidence of having received power from the Holy Spirit.

That is *Stephen's* story.

Now let's look at the second man in this breaking drama. He, too, is one of the greatest figures of the first century. In many ways this man is very much like Stephen. Like Stephen, he is a foreigner. He has come to Jerusalem to study, to sit under the great theologians of his century, especially Gamaliel. His home town is Tarsus, Celicia, a country about 300 miles to the north.

When Saul first left Tarsus and arrived in Jerusalem to become a seminary student, he most likely took up room and board with two of his relatives, Andronicus and Junias. Right now let us say he is around twenty-nine years old. (Don't forget that.) He is a devout Jew, a religious zealot without equal.

While studying at the temple seminary, Saul indignantly watched the Jesus sect (known as "the way") grow larger and larger—and in the Holy City, of all places! He discussed this abomination with his fellow students and listened daily as the nation's religious leaders became more and more upset.

The tolerance among the Jewish religious leaders toward *"the way"* was deteriorating almost by the hour! Saul saw some of his fellow students converted to Christ; he watched as even temple priests became believers. (Stephen had probably been the instrument behind some of these conversions.) The flame of Saul's anger was almost out of control. Temple priests! Following Jesus! Unthinkable! Finally, even his very own relatives, Andronicus and Junias, turned to Christ.

Perhaps it was *this* incident which pushed Saul past his breaking point.

At this same time the religious leaders of Judaism had also reached their breaking point. The fact that priests from among their own ranks were being converted meant that things were serious. *Empty pews among the devout!* If the Jewish leaders got just one good excuse, they were going to unleash a purge on these heretics. Even if someone had to *invent* the excuse to do it.

One more thing was sure: if the fire ever did fall on the followers of Christ, Saul would be there fanning the blaze.

Saul and Stephen are about to meet. When they do, heaven, earth and hell will tremble. Their clash will cause repercussions for 1900 years.

12

The Debate

Stephen made his way through the streets of Jerusalem. He was on his way to a debate. It was to be held in a large, gleaming stone building made of white marble.

Once inside you could quickly see the building was round; near the center of the room was a circle of marble pillars supporting a balcony. This balcony was reserved for women and was used mostly on the Sabbath. The ground floor had small benches pressed around the wall and loosely placed in other parts of the room. At the front of the room, which was probably opposite the door, sat a wood table. On the table was a wooden chest full of the ancient Hebrew scrolls, portions of the Scripture.

This was the Libertine Synagogue. It had been built by donations from a group of wealthy, foreign Jews. Throughout the week this synagogue served as a gathering place for foreign Jews who were visiting in the city. Here the Hellenic Jews could have Sabbath meetings in their native Greek language; in fact, all activity that went on here, throughout the entire week, was carried on in Greek.

The Libertine Synagogue was the national gathering place for all Greek speaking Jews. It was used not only for Sabbath meetings but also for informal discussions and lectures on the Scripture. From time to time it even became the scene of a debate. These debates were usually between two men, over some religious issues or interpretations of the Scripture.

Of late, because of Stephen, these debates had become the city's main attraction.

What brought on these debates between Stephen and his fellow Hellenic Jews?

It all had its beginning when Stephen started proclaiming the Gospel and healing the sick. Some of the Jews who heard him, challenged him as he spoke. The final outcome of their challenges was a number of full dress debates held here in the Libertine Synagogue. Soon Stephen had been challenged by, and had debated with, men from Cyrene, Alexandria, Asia Minor and even Saul's home country of Cilicia.

It appears the crowd came in increasing numbers to hear these debates. Stephen had unceremoniously turned the Libertine Synagogue, of all places, into a sounding board for the Gospel! It may be that even some of his challengers were converted to Christ! Stephen trounced every man who squared off with him.

For the orthodox Jews this was just too much. A follower of Jesus besting the finest minds in Jerusalem, and some contenders even converted—right here in the Libertine Synagogue!

The man had to be stopped. Permanently. By fair means or foul. The religious system had taken all it was going to take from Stephen, the Apostles and "the way." Gamaliel's advice would just have to be laid aside. Stephen and his heresy had to go.

Some of the zealots hatched a plot against Stephen's life. It went something like this: they would begin by spreading false rumors about this heretic; they would misquote him, twisting his words to make him sound guilty of blasphemy. If they could charge him with blasphemy, he could be brought to trial; if convicted (and by means of false witness they would see that he *was* convicted) he could be sentenced to death.

The only question was, when would be the best time to spring the trap. Apparently they decided the best time would be during one of the debates. Simply enough, one of them would declare he had heard Stephen blaspheme, and at that point they could take him. The Sanhedrin and the whole orthodox Jewish community was already astir with rumors, so arrest and trial would swiftly follow. If the plot worked, Stephen's doom was certain.

Who debated Stephen on that fateful day? No one knows. But all indications are that it was Saul.

If so, the scene unfolded this way.

Saul had stood by and watched as Stephen trounced his colleagues again and again. Finally, he could take it no longer. He challenged Stephen to verbal war. A date was set for them to clash.

When Stephen arrived for the debate, the Libertine Synagogue must have been packed. Everyone knew this debate would represent the best of two worlds: the world of theology *versus* the world of knowing Christ. Even the women's balcony was probably filled.

On the main floor the elders sat near the wall behind the table; the benches were all filled; the floor space was jammed. The room tingled with an air of expectation.

The time had come.

Saul stood. He was dressed in a blue-fringed robe. On his head was a turban, and fastened to it was the amulet, both signs of the proud sect of the Pharisees. (Saul was an unwitting tool in the plot on Stephen's life.)

Stephen stood. He was dressed in the simple garb of Jerusalem's poor.

The two men turned and faced one another; they walked over and stood either directly in front of the elders or in the center of the great round room.

We do not know the specific topic of their debate, but we do know the general format that debates followed in those days. One man would begin by simply asking his opponent a question. Sometimes it would be a long, involved question which revealed his own view; sometimes it was a short question with a hidden purpose. The second man would then answer the question and, in turn, ask his opponent a question. This was a method referred to as *diatribe*. Traditionally, when the debate was over, everyone in the room was to lay aside his own view on the topic and cast a vote for the man who had presented the stronger case.

The debate began.

We can only imagine the mounting drama of the next few hours. What those two men said, the give and take, all this is lost to us. But we do know that when the debate ended there was no question who had won.

Saul had zeal; Stephen had power. Saul had towering reason, logic, intellect; Stephen had wisdom. Saul knew the Scriptures; Stephen knew Christ. Saul was full of tradition and legalism; Stephen was full of grace and the Holy Spirit. Saul was filled with death; Stephen was filled with the Life of God.

It may have been just as the two men drew the debate to an end that someone decided the perfect moment to strike had finally come.

On cue an accuser jumped to his feet and began yelling to the startled crowd. "Blasphemer! Blasphemer! I have heard this man blaspheme!"

This was the signal.

Others, who had been waiting for this moment, jumped to their feet shouting and railing at Stephen, repeating the same accusation. Then more men were on their feet, followed by still others. Disorder broke out. Stephen was suddenly grabbed and dragged outside. The zealots raced him through the streets. They were on their way to the Sanhedrin. Stephen was about to be officially charged with blasphemy against God and Moses.

The holocaust had begun.

13

Seventy-One Men on Trial

The doors to the Hall of Polished Stones swing open.

All serious religious matters are tried here in the highest courtroom of the land. This is the "senate chamber" where the Sanhedrin meets. The whole Hall is stirring with activity.

This chamber is located inside the Temple grounds. Eight years ago Jesus was put on trial for His life here. Peter and John once stood here. Today it is Stephen; he is about to be tried for his life. The charge is blasphemy against God and Moses.

Just about a year ago, when the twelve Apostles were tried in this room, the Council just barely backed down from executing them. They were spared that day—thanks to Gamaliel. But today the Council's mood is different. This time they face only one relatively unknown man (although they know he will not remain unknown if he is not stopped!)

With a little imagination we can piece together the whole scene.

Stephen is led to the very center of the room and then left there alone, facing the Sanhedrin. The president of the Sanhedrin enters. He is the High Priest, a direct descendant of Aaron. Today he is in full dress: turban, tunic, jeweled breast-plate and all. He takes his place in the center of the great long curving bench which reaches half way around the wall of the room. Seated on either side of him are seventy judges. (These seventy men are the equivalent of both a United States senator and a Roman Catholic cardinal; their power is both religious and political.) At each end of the bench sits a recording secretary with his quill and papyrus to write down every word.*

On the opposite side of this circular room is another bench like the one on which the Sanhedrin is seated. Sitting on this bench, facing the Sanhedrin, are lawyers, teachers, court servants and future candidates for the Sanhedrin. One of the men seated there is the zealous young Pharisee, Saul of Tarsus. In the lonely center between these two benches stands the silent figure of Stephen.

The room is electric with tension.

Stephen, like Jesus Christ, like the Apostles, and like men before him and like other men since him, stands face to face with the religious system. No matter what religion it is, no matter what nation, no matter what age, the organized, entrenched religious system will do anything necessary to preserve itself when threatened. And Stephen, like the Lord Jesus and the Apostles before him, had definitely threatened *this* religious system.

Stephen waits quietly in the center of the room. His very demeanor unnerves everyone who dares glance his way. He is utterly calm; there is a sense of serene tranquility about him that defies description or comprehension. His strong face is peaceful, even radiant.

The charges are read; then the "witnesses" come forward. Each one stands and testifies that the charges brought against Stephen are true. Stephen has clearly preached and taught that Jesus the Nazarene is the Lord God! Their many testimonies come to an end.

By age old custom, the defendant is now allowed to answer for himself any charge brought against him.

The High Priest addresses Stephen directly. "Are these charges true?" Every eye in the room turns and fastens upon Stephen. How strange! His face is shining like the face of an angel. He pauses only briefly before he begins to speak. It is an address that Heaven has ordained. What Stephen says

---

*This court had jurisdiction over Jews in religious matters in almost the whole Palestinian area. They had little civil power. Execution of civil government was in the hands of the Romans, specifically in the hands of the procurator, a kind of governor, sent to Judea from Rome. They had no legal power to put a man to death.

today will be heard by *the very men* who crucified the Lord eight years ago. His words are less his own defense than a defense of his Lord. In fact, today Stephen will act as a lawyer defending his Lord eight years after *His* trial, when no man was present to defend Him!!

He begins.

It is obvious to everyone that he does not care at all for his own life. He makes no effort to defend himself or to gain sympathy for himself in answering the charges. Gradually it becomes apparent that Stephen has somehow turned the tables: he has put the Sanhedrin on trial . . . before Heavenly councils. None of the listeners can escape the reach of this incredible young man's words. They inwardly marvel at his calm, his eloquence, his boldness, his grasp of the history of God's dealings with man, and at his sheer power.

As Stephen recounts the whole saga of God's purpose and plan for this earth and for man, a recurring theme begins to emerge: God's desire has always been to have a people who would bear His image and have His authority; so over and over again throughout history, God has had to find a people, separate them from the world, and make them *His* people. God could then begin to work among those people. But with the passing of time, those very people, the very vessel which God had chosen, would begin to turn from Him and even to reject Him. Then God would decide to move afresh. At that point His *former* work would actually rise up to resist His *new* work. Over and again, stated Stephen, it happened the same way. God's former people reject not only His next new working, but they also reject the men whom God has sent to do His work.

As Stephen continues his declaration, everyone begins to see where he is going.

He is moving relentlessly toward present history, to the Sanhedrin's rejection of Jesus Christ. Stephen's hearers become fully aware that *he* is accusing *them* of opposing God! It is an outrage! Although it is against Jewish custom to interrupt a man giving a defense for his life, that is exactly what this audience wishes to do. They do have one way of showing Stephen their contempt for him: they begin to grind their teeth. Everyone in the room picks it up. While Stephen continues the room is filled with the low, dull sound of the grinding and gnashing of teeth.

Stephen nonetheless drives on with his point. He is oblivious to the rising expression of resentment. His words even became bolder as the tempo of the gnashing teeth intensifies. Both Stephen's message and the Jews' expression of hatred begin rising to an inevitable climax.

Stephen now fixes his gaze straightly upon the Sanhedrin; his voice ascends with authority; his words of judgment against the religious system fall like thunder.

"There has never been a prophet your predecessors in history did not persecute. They even killed some of God's own messengers. They killed the very men who announced the coming of His righteous Servant." The full power of Stephen's gaze now turns to the High Priest.

"And now *you* have even betrayed and murdered *Him!*" With one mighty sweep Stephen takes in the whole Sanhedrin as he reaches the crescendo of his declaration:

"*You* are the ones who received God's law, and the law handed down by angels. Yet *you* have not obeyed it."

The accused has become the accuser.

Stephen has charged the *Sanhedrin* with murder, the murder of God's elected One! The silence snaps. Suddenly everyone in the room is on his feet. They might have charged upon Stephen right then, but something about him suddenly stopped them. Stephen was standing in the middle of the room gazing at the ceiling, his whole being transfixed, his face glowing with the glory of God.

First century believers had a disconcerting way of stepping outside the confines of time and space. (It's not impossible, you know.) This was one of those holy moments.

Spellbound, Stephen stands innocently marvelling, oblivious to everyone else in the room. Suddenly he shouts out at what he is seeing.

"Look!"

"I see heaven; it is opened!! I see the Son of Man standing at the right hand of God."

That did it; the whole courtroom went wild.

Bedlam ensued, madness broke out. Men vaulted over

benches and chairs. Everyone in the room rushed toward Stephen, putting their hands over their ears as they went, a sign that they could not bear to hear another word of blasphemy from his mouth. It was a scene of utter insanity. All judicial dignity, form, and position dissolved. There was nothing in that room but a crowd gone wild, intent upon one thing: the death of Stephen.

Stephen was grabbed, pulled, and dragged all at once. The chaotic mass eventually began to move in one direction, gaining speed as it went. Every man in the room knew where he was headed. They spilled out the door, pushing, howling and screaming as they surged forward. They poured down the steps and raced out across the broad "Court of the Priests," into the sunlight, down more steps, pouring madly through one court after another, screaming like attacking warriors as they went. Their number swelled as bystanders and sightseers ran after them, not certain why, but sure that there was excitement aplenty behind this judicial riot.

Out of the temple area, along the streets of Jerusalem, the furious crowd moved.

They catapulted through the north gate and raced full speed toward "The Place of Execution." Their pace was not even slowed as they approached the small pit-like arena called the Rock of Execution. The banister around the pit was all that stopped them as they piled into one another. Stephen was hurled over the wall into the eleven foot pit below.

This was *not* the way a man was supposed to be stoned.

Before being cast into the pit, the convicted man was first supposed to be tied hand and foot, and then thrown head first, down into the pit. There, while still unconscious, he was to be stoned by those who witnessed against him.

But Stephen had been convicted of nothing and the insane mob had not had time or mind to recall this preliminary ritual. Stephen, having not been tied, landed feet first. He stood, turned around, and looked straight up into the face of the now stunned mob. A moment of sanity must have ensued. Perhaps a second of silence swept the crowd as men regained their senses and tried to think what to do next. What *could* they do in this unusual situation?

The moment of hesitation passed.

Someone motioned to the witnesses. Quickly they pushed their way to the banister around the arena. It was *their* duty to cast the first stones. The stones were large. The witnesses began stripping off their outer cloaks. One witness looked around for someone to guard his cloak while he proceeded with his task. He recognized Saul standing nearby, recalled his total commitment to the death of Stephen and, as a symbol of Saul's compliance, handed his cloak to him. The other witnesses caught the meaning of the gesture and also laid their garments at Saul's feet.

As the witnesses raised the heavy stones above their heads and hurled them down into the pit, the first martyr of church history very simply slipped to his knees and fell quietly asleep.

14
Elegy in Tears

The arena was empty. The last of the mob had gone. The only evidence left of the riot was the lifeless form at the bottom of the pit.

Soon, a small group of men made their way cautiously to the edge of the arena. They gazed down in horror at the sight below. Before them was something never before seen - a believer who had give his life for the Lord! The men quietly slipped down into the pit. Tenderly, even reverently, they lifted the body out and carried it away. As they departed they wept bitterly. Theirs were deep, convulsive tears of grief. After all, Stephen had been the inspiration and admiration of all the believers who had been saved that glorious Pentecostal day.

Why were their tears bitter, their grief so great? Stephen had been special to them; to all the church in Jerusalem he was unique. He was a "recent" believer, not like the Apostles who had physically followed Jesus. Yet Stephen had grown into a giant before the very eyes of the church. Because of him everyone had great expectations for the future of the church. Because of Stephen the future looked as promising as the past. All the believers had watched Stephen speak and heal; for one brief moment they had thought that God was raising up a "second group" of men, a group of men to come *after* the Apostles who would be as *capable* as the Apostles. Stephen *seemed* to be the first of a new breed of men!

Now he was dead.

Let us look at Stephen's special significance to the church. To see how special Stephen really was you have to go back and see how special the twelve Apostles had been. At the time the Apostles were raised up, they too, were a "new breed" of men. In fact, in all history there had never been a group of men like the twelve. They were special for only one reason: they had lived in the actual presence of the Lord for nearly four years!! No one else in human history could claim that experience!

What was it like to constantly live in the presence of Christ? One thing is sure: it had radically transformed those twelve men. There were no other men like them on the earth. Certainly no one else could say as they did, "I have spent over 20,000 hours living, breathing and walking in the presence of Jesus Christ."

Think of it: over 20,000 hours spent in the presence of God! *That* one fact and that alone is what really made the twelve! Living each of those hours in the presence of Christ is the first of many ingredients which went into the lives of these men to make them Apostles.

(Let us consider our own day. We need to see Apostleship restored! But if we are to have *true* Apostles on this earth again, then one thing *must* come first: a staggering, unbelievable number of hours spent in the Lord's presence! We can accept no cheap substitute for Apostleship.)

Just look at what 20,000 hours with Christ did to those twelve men: it purified them in motive, in deed and in thought. Probably we have never seen men so pure in heart, so purged of hidden motives. During their time with Christ, a great storehouse of divinity was deposited in them. They were divine *men*.

So what were the twelve? Men purged in motive, pure in being, divine in character. They were men who lived in the conscious presence of Christ. Furthermore, the Apostles had developed a "habit" during over three years with Jesus—the habit of *always* being in the Lord's presence—and they *kept* the habit even after He ascended! Is that impossible? No, it is not. Eight years after Pentecost the Apostles were still experiencing that same intimate relationship with Christ. They were *still* living constantly in His presence.

(In fact, their relationship with Christ was even deeper, far deeper than even living in the Lord's presence, but it is not the purpose of this book to explore the depths found in knowing Christ.)

So the first century church had twelve men who knew how to live in the presence of Christ.

Even so, the church still had a problem. It was really neat having those twelve men around, with all their wonderful, incredible experience with Christ. But what about the other believers? The Lord was gone. Could they *who had come later* also share the deep, rich, spiritual experience of the twelve Apostles? Could they too "live" with Christ? Could *they* know Him? That was a big question in the first century.

(The question is even bigger today. Today, without the physical Christ, today without twelve Apostles, today with church life and the deep, inward experience of Christ being virtually lost, will anything like the twelve ever appear again? Will there ever be men who live in constant, unbroken fellowship with Christ? What a glorious question!)

That brings us back to Stephen.

Stephen was unique. He was the "yes" to that question. He was the first visible evidence that *men* of the stature and experience of the *twelve* might continue to be raised up by the Lord. But Stephen was "one of a kind." There were twelve men in that "first" group; there was only one man in the "second group." But though that "second group" had only one man in it, at least it was a sign that maybe, just maybe, others like him would begin to appear. The fact that there was one man like Stephen gave hope.

Stephen was unlike anyone else in all human history!! He had never met Christ; he had *never* even *seen* Him. He could never claim, as the Apostles could, that he had lived in the Lord's physical presence for over three years. Stephen had an altogether different history. He had become a convert to Jesus Christ through the Apostles. He had given his life utterly to the Lord. He had lived in the rich experience of the church every day. And then, little by little, he too had begun to live in the presence of the Lord—the Lord's Spirit. No, it was not a constant walk in the *conscious* presence of the Lord, *not at first*. But it did grow into a constant walk.

How did Stephen come to such a point in his life?

Did he have an advantage over us? He surely did!! He had the Apostles. They had lived in the Lord's presence. They knew what it was like to live in the Lord's presence, and they told him about it. But Stephen should *not* have that advantage over us. There ought to be men living today who can sit down and speak of their first-hand experience of living in the presence of Christ.

Gradually, Stephen had learned to live more and more in the presence of the Lord. He gave the Lord more hours of his day. Then he gave more and more *whole* days to Him. Like the Apostles, Stephen became rich in his knowledge and experience of the indwelling Christ. Stephen became well acquainted with God!

How, exactly, did Stephen learn from the Apostles? This way: for four or five hours per day, six days a week, the Apostles talked, proclaimed, and taught the church in Jerusalem about Jesus Christ. And Stephen had the privilege of sitting there to hear what they said, obeying what they instructed. The Apostles' ministry probably lasted *at least* four hours per day, six days a week for eight years. Figure that up! It totals over 9,000 hours of Apostolic ministry which Stephen received! Over 9,000 hours of revelation from men who had experienced Christ personally! Over 9,000 hours from twelve men who spoke mostly about "living in the presence of Jesus Christ" or things even deeper than that!

This is the advantage Stephen had which you have never had!

Furthermore, Stephen could walk up to these men and ask them questions. They were real, living people, standing right in front of him. He could listen to twelve human beings talk of their *own* frustrations, their thick-headedness, their slow grasp of spiritual things, their total failures, and—at last—of their gradual, growing insight into *Him.*

In a word, Stephen learned, for himself, *how* to live in the Lord's presence; he learned how to live by divine life; and he learned it from those who had themselves lived in the Lord's presence and who now lived by His life! *Herein* is perhaps the greatest missing element, the overlooked secret of the early church. There are, as you are beginning to see, many, many things the early believers did which we do not do today. (And many things we do that they *never* did!) And all of those wonderful experiences of the first century must be regained.

Still, of all the things the early believers knew and experienced, nothing is quite as important to us as seeing recovered the simple matter of a deep, constant, daily experience of Christ. This deep fellowship of His presence was the mainstay of the early church. Being dealt with by the cross, living by a life *not* human, living in oneness with God: here is the place to dig!

All of our present day schemes, programs, visions, buildings, institutions, Scriptural understanding, insights, knowledge and everything else are just tinsel—just useless, dead weight—in the light of the experience of knowing the Lord and walking in the sense of His presence.

There was another thing Stephen had going for him besides the ministry of the Apostles which men today do not have.

Stephen was surrounded by 20,000 believers who were after the same thing he was after! Wherever he went, whomever he met, whomever he talked to, every person he knew, every person with whom he spent any time, *was after exactly the same thing* he was after: to live a practical, normal, everyday life, yet live it in constant fellowship with Christ! That is church life! That is Stephen's second advantage over you!

That was Stephen's secret.

Stephen had no concept, like ours, of "going to church." There was no such thing in the first century as going to church. Church was not a place, but a way of life. He met with believers early in the morning, before dawn. When he got home from work later in the day, the first thing he saw was a house full of believers. The afternoon was spent talking and fellowshipping with them and hearing the Apostles at Solomon's Porch. The evenings were spent with other believers again. And all that time Stephen and everyone with him were pursuing the same thing: unbroken fellowship with Christ.

The church was never something those people went to. They *were* the church! The purpose of their moment by moment life was to live together *by Christ.* Everything anyone said, everything anyone did, was toward the goal of experiencing Jesus Christ. And that was where Stephen lived.

That was the kind of atmosphere he grew up in. He lived *in* the church. He was surrounded day and night by people with a passion for knowing Jesus Christ.

That is what Stephen had going for him.

That is what the Lord intended for you *to have going for* you!

Put these two factors, the Apostles and church life, together and you see why Stephen was Stephen. These are enormous assets when it comes to the daily business of being a follower of Jesus Christ! (And God intended that they be *normal* assets for every child of His.) Can you imagine what it would be like to live all the time with people who had but one desire: to know Christ, to know Him personally, to know Him intimately and to *live* in His presence?

Now you can begin to see what it was that made Stephen the first of a new breed of men; a breed *very much* like the twelve Apostles themselves . . . yet distinctly different from them. Stephen had never met Christ in the flesh. Without ever seeing Him he had actually come to know Christ as intimately as the Apostles knew Him!

Stephen was proof that the twelve would *not* be the last men of true spiritual stature.

But now Stephen was gone! The hopes of the church were shattered.

Now you can understand why those brothers who carried away Stephen's body wept so bitterly. Yes, it was because they had loved him dearly, but more than that, they had seen in him a future hope for the church. They had seen in him the first evidence of one who *knew* Christ well though he had never *seen* Him! These hopes were now dashed, and they wept bitterly. They wept because the enemy had stamped out their hope. It was a crushing defeat.

Little did they realize the power of God. At that very moment, even while they buried this one, the Lord was working to raise up more men. That second group, that "new breed," would yet be born. Not only was God going to raise up a new group, but He would also thrust them out to do a new work, one that would parallel, and even exceed, the deeds of the Apostles!

Those who took Stephen's body out to bury it did not realize that God had *other* men of Stephen's stature in the Jerusalem church! No one knew who they were. Nonetheless, they *were* there. There were a group of men in the church who were as capable, and as prepared, and as ready to go, as the Apostles had been on the day of Pentecost. This would soon become evident.

But keep this in mind: it took eight years to get them ready. If you overlook that, you overlook the key. Eight years . . . eight years in church life.

It has been a bloody morning. It began with Stephen's trial, and was followed with his death by stoning. Devout and saddened men have buried him. But the day is far from over. Stephen is not the only believer who will shed his blood on this black day.

This dark, bloody day has only begun.

15

Holocaust

Stephen had been dead only a matter of hours, yet the Hall of Polished Stones was again filling. The Sanhedrin had no time to spare. They meant to act swiftly—before the news of Stephen's death had a chance to spread throughout the city. They planned to settle this whole issue in a matter of days if at all possible.

Their strategy was very simple: they would launch a city-wide, door to door search-and-arrest for all followers of Jesus. They would jail every one of them. The charge would be the same as Stephen's: blasphemy. If a disciple was found guilty he would either be stoned, beaten or imprisoned.

The Sanhedrin knew that the use of stoning was almost out of the question. In order to *legally* stone a person to death, it was necessary to get written permission from the Roman government. This was a hard thing to come by, especially if it was over religious matters. The Sanhedrin knew the Romans might grant a few such requests, but not many. In order to stop "the way" they would have to rely mostly on surprise, terror and brutality.

What the Sanhedrin needed most of all was a man to lead their purge: a man who would be swift and thorough, who would catch the disciples off guard and then rain down enough terror and spread enough fear to send everyone into a panic. They hoped to see a wholesale renunciation of Jesus Christ. The Sanhedrin looked around for the best man to do this grizzly job. Their choice? Saul! He was literally breathing hatred against "the way."

With that appointment made, guardsmen were soon scurrying up and down city streets and rushing unannounced into hundreds of homes. Presently a multitude of believers were being unceremoniously hauled out of their homes and hustled into jail. Many were beaten and handled cruelly in the process.

Saul allowed for no delay.

Word of what was happening shot through the city. Little by little the believers became aware of what was happening. They had never faced a crisis like this before. This was the *first* persecution of the body of Christ in church history. Everyone was caught completely off guard; the number of those arrested and facing trial was swelling by the hour. Saul had even started trying disciples in court . . . and the worst was not over yet! Mayhem reigned.

To fully understand what happened next, we need to see what was happening to the disciples who had already been arrested. Let us, then, follow the steps of just one disciple who had been arrested, and see exactly what happened to him.*

Once soldiers had entered a home and arrested a disciple he was probably taken to the Libertine synagogue where Saul seems to have set up a courtroom.

A little stunned, the disciple sits quietly, awaiting his turn to face Saul. Perhaps at first he feels apprehensive, but his apprehension gradually gives way to a deep calm. All the inward experiences which this brother has had with Christ over the past eight years have prepared him for this hour. A sense of peace and courage begins to flow into his spirit.

At last his turn comes. He is escorted to the center of the room. Seated behind some wooden tables a few feet away are Saul and the synagogue elders. One of them states the charge, "blasphemy against Moses and against God." How has he blasphemed? By professing that Jesus is the Messiah, the Son of God. The elders (or Saul) probably explained that this charge would be dropped immediately if he would prove that it was not true. More than likely they explained exactly *how* he could satisfy the court that the charges were false: all he had to do was to declare, "Jesus is not the Messiah." (Perhaps their demands were tougher than that, perhaps they demanded that he state with his own mouth: "Jesus is cursed." To the ear of a disciple, *this* statement was blasphemy!)

*The disciple is imaginary, the proceedings are not.

112

Would this disciple deny that Christ was the Son of God? Would he curse the name of the Lord?

If the disciple would deny his Lord, he would be free. If he held to his confession, he faced the *certainty* of a brutal whipping, the *probability* of imprisonment, and the *possibility* of death by stoning. (There is no question that some disciples must have crumbled under such pressure.)

The disciple stands before them in silence—just as his Lord once stood at a similar trial in this same city eight years ago. The elders can break that silence by "adjuring" the disciple to answer. In such a case the faithful disciple can only respond, "I will not deny my Lord."

But there was something else the disciple could do at this point, just before the court handed down its decision of guilt. He could state simply to the court: "I have something to say in my defense." This was a very short, very simple sentence, but one that had long been honored in Hebrew history. The tribunal was honor bound to let the disciple speak.

The Lord had once warned His followers that a day was coming when they would be hauled into synagogues for the sake of His name. He had told them to relax: He would give them the words to speak. That time had now come for this disciple.

He swallows hard and, taking his Lord's word by faith, opens his mouth and lets his tongue speak. Soon he is listening to himself make a startling and powerful declaration of his faith, backed by infallible proof of the deity of his Lord.

Saul had to sit there and listen. It was like tangling with Stephen all over again!

(In the days to come Saul would hear it again and again, from the rich, from the poor, the educated, the illiterate. People who simply did not have the ability to speak would stand before him and declare with the boldness of an archangel that Jesus was Lord! Those were frightening words to Saul. The fires of hate in his bosom grew even hotter.)

Over and again the court would have to hear these very moving, first-hand testimonies. It is possible, even in this black hour of defeat, that people were being converted to Christ by the boldness and testimony of the Lord's unlettered disciples.

113

The disciple finishes his testimony. Saul quickly polls the elders, and the verdict is made. The accused is found guilty. The sentence: "a beating, thirty-nine lashes. Then imprisonment."

What were the "thirty-nine lashes?" They were a punishment just this side of stoning. In fact, the "forty stripes less one" were sometimes fatal. It was a type of beating employed only among the Jewish religious community. Its purpose was to bring an erring Hebrew back to the orthodox views of Judaism, that is, back to the teaching of Moses and the traditions of the elders. It was a severe punishment administered to bring the accused to repentance. It had probably been invented as a last ditch show of mercy to be used on a man in *place* of stoning him to death.

To be sentenced to this lashing was the most shameful thing that could happen to a Jew. It brought shame not only upon him but also upon his entire family. In that day a man apparently would have done anything to escape the physical agony and the social humiliation of these stripes. That was about to change . . . and very suddenly! The followers of Jesus Christ showed no sign of shame. Instead, they stood there rejoicing! It was very unnerving . . . and probably unprecedented in all human history.

The disciple listens to the sentence. His face glowing, like Stephen's, he is led to stand between two marble columns. His hands are spread apart and tied to the pillars. Then his back is stripped bare. A few feet behind him someone places a stand. Another man in another part of the room stands and strides over to the stand. He is the "hazzan." As he steps up onto the stand, he unrolls a heavy whip. The whip has four strips of leather on it, each about three or four feet long. Two of these leather strips are of calf's hide, the other two are from the hide of a donkey.

The hazzan, standing on the small raised platform, turns slowly around toward the bared back of the disciple. The disciple cannot see the proceedings, but knows what is about to happen. The hazzan raises the whip high into the air, straightens and then brings it down with all his might.

The whip does not land on the disciple's back, but, rather, on the top of his shoulders. The leather strips reach out beyond his shoulders, falling hard upon his chest and stomach. The blow instantly causes welts and bruises all over

114

his chest and stomach. The hazzan quickly pulls the whip back with a jerk and the leather rakes back over the bruised skin.

There is a pause. Again the whip goes high into the air, and again it comes straight down upon the disciple's shoulders. This time the leather lands upon tender, swollen skin. With each blow the disciple's skin becomes more bruised. The welts begin opening and finally turn into open gashes. After even more blows, the leather starts finding its way into the bone of the rib cage. Each blow is like coals of burning fire upon the chest.

The disciple receives thirteen such lashes across his front. At this point he is probably already in shock, dehydrated and nearly delirious with pain. The inquisitor now begins the second thirteen lashes, aiming them at the back. Thirteen slashes of leather find their way across the right side of the disciple's back, each furrowing deeper into the flesh than the one before.

By now the disciple is probably semi-conscious and on the verge of fainting. His muscle coordination is lost. No longer able to stand, he now half swings from the cords binding him to the marble pillars. And there are still thirteen more lashes to come. These make their permanent mark on his left side.

At last it is over.

This brave believer, probably unconscious and close to death, is cut down and dragged out. (Almost unquestionably, in the following few days, some will die from these beatings.)

Saul watched. He could never have dreamed that one day his own body would carry 195 such scars.

The disciple had made it through the ordeal. He did not deny his Lord, and he had the glorious privilege of fellowship in the sufferings of his Lord. From the synagogue he was probably carried to an awaiting prison. There he undoubtedly passed out from pain. When he awakened, his body would be on fire and he would have an unquenchable thirst. Moving would be agony. Ahead of him would be weeks of slow healing and intense pain. Across his chest, across his stomach and across his back he would forever carry deep furrowed scars as trophies of his love for his Lord.

It was a shocking scene. Saul's plan called for the arrest and trial of 20,000 people—all to face the same ordeal. There was to have been no distinction of gender. Women faced the possibility of this same agony.

Darkness finally arrived. The long day of injustice, death and terror was coming to an end. It had been the blackest day in Jerusalem since the crucifixion of Christ eight years earlier. The next day promised to be even bloodier.

As night finally came, a remarkable thing began to happen. We do not know if it was spontaneous or if the twelve Apostles passed along the word; we only know that a truly astounding thing took place that night in Jerusalem.

The church in Jerusalem began to vanish!

Very quietly, in homes all over the city, believers began gathering up a few belongings and bidding one another a deep and affectionate good-bye, and then slipping out into the darkness. Before dawn, hundreds, perhaps thousands of believers had departed from the city. The next dawn found the roads leading out of Jerusalem spotted with fleeing pilgrims.

In Jerusalem, however, the new day brought more horror. Those who had not fled the city found themselves hunted prey. Arrest procedures broke down completely. Any believer who was found, man or woman, was bodily dragged through the streets. It was obvious to everyone that there was no wisdom whatsoever in remaining in town. So all began to leave.

Within a matter of days there was not a believer left in the city. All 20,000 had fled. The city was literally devoid of anyone who professed to be a follower of Jesus Christ.*

Overnight, the church in Jerusalem had ceased to exist!

Imagine! At the end of eight years there was not even one church on this earth. The one *and only* church, the church in Jerusalem, had come to an end.

Did this mean that the enemy had won? Had the Sanhedrin triumphed over the body of Christ? Had the *past*

---

*The twelve Apostles, alone, elected to stay in Jerusalem. It appears they were in hiding; the authorities obviously did not know they were still in town.

work of God triumphed over the new work of God? Had Saul stopped the Kingdom of Jesus Christ?

The guardians of the religious system had moved to destroy the church, to obliterate it from the face of the earth; but unwittingly, they had not stopped the church, they had launched it!

16

100 New Churches

There were only a few roads leading out of Jerusalem into the 200 towns, cities and villages of Judea.* During that long night after Stephen's death, those roads were dotted continuously with followers of Christ fleeing the capital.

You can imagine what it was like that day. A disciple would come to a fork in the road, pause a moment, and seek to choose which direction he would go. How did he make his decision? One disciple might remember that he had friends and relatives in a certain town. Another disciple would go a different direction—knowing that a certain town offered a better chance to get a job. Still another, having no friends or relatives in either Judea or Galilee, had to stand at that fork in the road, bow his head and make his decision according to an inner sense he received from the Lord.

By daybreak of the day after Stephen had been stoned, many of the disciples had probably already reached some of these outlying cities. Some remained in the first city they reached, there to make a new home. Others only rested there briefly and pushed on to cities further out. Hour after hour, day after day, the flow increased until Jerusalem was emptied of believers.

On the road disciples began bumping into one another. Others met in the market places and city streets. By every standard, such meetings should have been very sad. There should have been words of consolation. stories of "unfair

---

*The 200 towns are an archaeological estimate and include the provinces of both Judea and Galilee; those two areas share the same race, language, religion and culture . . . and are considered to be the same country in the eyes of the Jews, the Galileans being the less refined of the two

treatment," "tragic suffering," "pitiful situation," "wicked men," etc. By all rights those hours should have been a replay of the days just after the crucifixion: a people scattered and defeated. But the opposite was true: the accidental reunions along the road were moments of joy. Bursts of shouting and exultation went up instantly wherever the believers met. These were not ordinary people. They were a people who could not be defeated. They *could not* be defeated.

How is that possible? To answer that question you would have to experience the body life of the church for eight years. (Knowing church life would pretty well equip you to withstand virtually anything life could ever hope to throw at you!) But church life is not the only thing those people had going for them. They had an overpowering revelation of who Christ was. They knew Christ. They knew Him very well. They were saturated and permeated with *Him.* The ever triumphant Christ was constantly welling up in them. Circumstances did *not* affect that experience, regardless of what the circumstances were.

So watch the disciples as they stand there embracing one another! Something new and wonderful is being born. Believe it or not, spontaneously, unexpectedly and utterly without planning, *the evangelization of Judea is about to be launched!*

We do not know all the details of what took place during those dramatic days, but most of the story can be pieced together. Let us follow a few imaginary disciples.

In the middle of the night a disciple decides to flee Saul's wrath. He slips outside the city walls. On his second day out he meets up with another brother who is also fleeing Jerusalem. They embrace, shout, rejoice, and praise the Lord. They exchange stories, remembering they met before somewhere in Jerusalem. They discover they have mutual acquaintances in the Lord, and rejoice some more. They are both going in the same general direction. As they walk along, speaking of Christ, reminding one another of who they really are in Christ, well-springs of joy keep bursting forth. They are excited men. Soon they see a small town in the distance. They decide to stop there for a day or two. After that they plan to move on down the road to their destinations.

As they enter the town both men get a spontaneous urge. They want to tell the people in that town just what is happening upon this earth. As they walk inside the gates they begin stopping people and telling them what has been going on in Jerusalem. Gradually they move on toward the center of the city, to the market place. At first they go around from person to person, telling the news of what has happened to them in the last few days. Soon they have expanded their story to what has happened in the past eight fantastic years. The people listening recall that ten years earlier they had seen and heard Jesus pass through this very town. Soon the two men are not talking to one or two people, but instead, to a group.

This is a new experience for them. It had always been the Apostles who had done daring, aggressive things. But one of them, delighted at this brand new experience, raises his volume to be better heard by everyone. Soon there is more volume and more listening ears. Suddenly he announces—to his own surprise—that he is going to return to the market place that afternoon and explain further what the Lord has been doing. "Spread the word. Bring your neighbors," he hears himself telling his listeners.

A fair-sized afternoon crowd shows up that day in the market place. Some of the listeners are even converted! Still others want to hear more. Nearly everyone present shows some kind of interest.

The disciples have a change in plans. They decide to extend their stay in this town.

It was in just such a simple way that the proclamation of the Gospel in Judea began. The Gospel was permanently established in Judea, not by the Lord who had once visited these very cities a decade ago, nor by the twelve Apostles with their reputation for proclaiming the Gospel. No, the Gospel was established in Judea by ordinary, untrained, untutored men who came into town, stood in the market, and proclaimed the Gospel of Christ. They were simple, ordinary people, common laborers and tradesmen. They were "the faces in the crowd" who met in Solomon's Porch and gathered in the homes of Jerusalem. These men had never received any training to prepare them for evangelizing Judea. Furthermore, they had never done anything for Christ before today. But there was a fire in their bosoms. The Gospel burst out of their hearts with a passion.

This scene was being repeated in other towns throughout the whole area.

Judea was rocked on its heels.

How was the church born in Judea? Perhaps like this.

Other disciples fleeing Jerusalem heard the local gossip as they were passing through. So, for sure, they headed straight for the market place to hear their brothers uncork the Gospel.

It is not difficult to imagine that as those men stood there proclaiming the Gospel to a crowd, they were suddenly interrupted by a "Hallelujah" or an "Amen" from somewhere down the street as other disciples came running into the square. At that moment something was being born. By this kind of coincidence the disciples were "discovering" one another, and out of their accidental encounters the first meeting of the church in that new city was born!!

It was this simple, unplanned process—declaring the Gospel in the market place, winning some listeners to Christ, creating a place of rendezvous for other believers coming into town—that God used over and over as His instrument to give birth to the church. The Jerusalem church was being transplanted all over Judea!

So, in a few days, the church was gathering in that town . . . meeting in homes. After a few more days, or maybe it was weeks, some of the pilgrims probably pushed on to the next city. Others decided to stay. They would be part of this fledgling church. Those who pushed on had caught the fever of spreading the Gospel.

By this time just about everyone fleeing Jerusalem had caught the disease. They were all proclaiming Christ at every wide place in the road.

They spoke Christ; they gossiped Christ; they met; they nurtured the new converts. What the Apostles had done before their eyes for eight years they now began to experience—in Judea. The church was born overnight in village after village and town after town.

Yes, the church had been snuffed out in one city—but it was being born in dozens more!

That is not all. As we shall see, not only was the church being born in cities and towns all over Judea, but men—giants—were also being born in the twinkling of an eye.

Let's meet one of those men!

The year is 38 a.d.

17

The Second Stephen

His name is Phillip.

In Jerusalem he had shared the same spiritual history as Stephen!

Stephen had signaled the beginning of a whole new breed of men, but Stephen was dead; the "new breed" had been snuffed out before it was born. Or was it? Suddenly, here was Phillip! Very much alive.

Phillip holds a unique place in church history. No other man can make his claim, for Phillip ushered in a new day.

Phillip had just lost a beloved brother in Christ. The death of Stephen, another of the *seven,* had doubtlessly stunned him. The evening of the day Stephen died it probably reached Phillip's ears that still other dear saints were being dragged through the streets and jailed. By nightfall he had seen the church in Jerusalem begin to dissolve. And, probably before daybreak, he had left everything on earth he owned and everyone he knew and had departed into Judea.

But Phillip was not even thinking of his loss. Christ was his everything. It was almost as though the persecution had never happened. Phillip had walked out the Jerusalem gates, not with an attitude of "we are defeated," or "woe is me," but rather thinking things like "you think you can stop us? Just watch!" Or perhaps it was: "Stand Back. There has been a blaze in my heart for years. At last I am going to get a chance to proclaim the wonder of knowing Christ!"

Phillip turned north when he left Jerusalem. The first major city he came to was Samaria. The Lord Jesus had been there about eleven years earlier and had stayed for a few days. As far as we know that was the only contact that city had ever had with the Gospel. Phillip entered Samaria with all cannons blazing, proclaiming the redemption of Christ. Throngs of people began pouring out to hear him.

What got all these people out?

Phillip was preaching the bone-crushing, custom-breaking, community-dividing, government-defying, outlawed, illegal, earthshaking, heaven-rattling, mind boggling *Gospel of the Kingdom!*

The Gospel of the Kingdom is a gospel so powerful that it will blow the cork right off the world system, the religious system, the conventions and the complacency of no matter what age, what nation, or what time or place. The Gospel of the Kingdom will *still* shake the foundation of nations. Yes, even in our day! Yes, even in nations that guarantee religious freedom. The Gospel of the Kingdom *sounds* like treason to the ears of unconverted men. (It isn't, but it surely sounds like it!)

But the Gospel of the Kingdom cannot be preached until there are men like Phillip who are qualified to preach it! Phillip sat under Apostles; he had eight years of the *pure* experience of church life, living almost constantly in the conscious presence of Christ; and, lastly, he had obeyed the Gospel of the Kingdom *before he spoke it.* (So you see, you may have to wait a little while before you can hear this message! It takes a certain kind of man to be able to proclaim it. Otherwise it's just not quite the Gospel of the Kingdom.)

Phillip's message, Phillip's power, rattled Samaria. Scores of people began responding to his message: they would know nothing but Christ. Then Phillip baptized them—a seal of their abandonment of the world. In the fervor and the freedom and the joy of that hour, while hundreds were rejoicing in their salvation, while the atmosphere was soaked with the power of God, Phillip even tried his hand at healing the sick. (Men will sometimes do foolish things like that in an hour that is burning with the Spirit!) Exactly how he began we do not know; all we know is that sometime during the glory of that hour, Phillip dared! He either tried to heal someone or to cast out a demon—something he had never done before in his long life as a believer. And God honored him! With that the flood-gates of heaven broke open! More healings occurred, more demons were cast out.

126

The whole place was filled with joy.

Samaria began to witness something akin to the time of Pentecost—but more. Samaria was having the same privilege Jerusalem once had when it witnessed Stephen burst out of the ranks aflame with the Gospel. Yes! It had happened again! But this time it was not Pentecost. This time it was not the Apostles. This time is was not even Stephen. This time it was Phillip! A man was proclaiming the Gospel who had never done so before in his life. He certainly had never healed anyone, either. Yet there he was! He was wielding the Gospel with astonishing power and with the full anointing of God. So, dear reader, that long period of waiting, "doing nothing," *does* pay off. Here is a second man to match the power of the Apostles, both in preaching the Gospel and in signs. Eight years in the church had *more* than paid off.

Samaria was rocked!

That new breed of men would yet be born. It had not been stamped out after all! Enemy, take note. World, beware. There is still hope that a new generation of men who can equal, or even surpass, the Apostles will yet fill the stage of this drama. And if the rest of this new breed turn out anything like Stephen and Phillip, the earth is in for a treat . . . and hell is in for a threat.

Word soon got back to the Apostles in Jerusalem about the awesome events in Samaria. (Though the Apostles were in hiding, messages were obviously getting to them.) A lot of wonderful news must have been coming in from other parts of Judea, but the report from Samaria really caught the Apostles' attention. This called for some special consideration. Some real *problems* could come out of this.

After all, Samaritans were not even Jews!

It was decided that Peter and John would go up to get a first hand look. When they arrived in Samaria things were as they had heard: the Samaritans were believers! At that moment the two Apostles did a significant thing. They laid hands on those half Jew, half gentile people. In so doing they added the blessing of the Holy Spirit and the blessing of their own hands to a despised race. They welcomed them into the church.

(It appears the Apostles were *often* called to cities throughout Judea to add their blessing to newly born

127

churches. But evidently this Apostolic blessing was not an absolute *necessity*. Maybe it was considered a necessity at that time, in 38 a.d. If so, the whole concept was blown sky high in 43 a.d., in a city far to the north!)

Out of the combined efforts of Phillip, Peter, and John, the church in Samaria was born.

The Apostles stayed in Samaria a few days. They joined Phillip in proclaiming the Gospel of the Kingdom; that must have been a triple treat indeed. Soon, though, they started back home for Jerusalem. By the way, that little trip up to Samaria marked the first time the Apostles did anything to indicate they might one day live out the so called "great commission." Until then they had spent eight years in one city! As they set out for home they seemed to have caught the spirit of the day. The two Apostles stopped at every town and village in Samaria they came to and, taking their signal from Phillip, proclaimed the Gospel. After nearly a decade, the Apostles finally had gone somewhere other than Jerusalem. (To the ends of the earth, maybe? No! Less than thirty miles!)

Take a quick glance at Judea and you realize just this same sort of story was happening everywhere.

Men were traveling up and down the roads of Judea, stopping at everything that even looked like a town and proclaiming the glories of Jesus Christ. A church was springing up in every city. These churches were made up partly of believers from Jerusalem and partly of new converts. The 20,000 fleeing disciples had suddenly turned into 20,000 burning witnesses to the Gospel. What was supposed to have been an hour of defeat had turned into an avalanche of joy, victory . . . and advance.

(Keep in mind that every one of these churches had people in them with previous experience in church life. Also, the twelve Apostles were beginning to make their appearance all over Judea. Point: there is no purely spontaneous church popping up here.)

After a period of time Phillip, too, left Samaria. How long he was there, raising up the church, we simply do not know. This we know: an angel told him to travel south again. This command he obeyed, getting as far south as Gaza, a strip of wilderness below Jerusalem. There he met a royal

Ethiopian courtier and pointed him to Christ. After that encounter Phillip turned west toward the Mediterranean Sea.

The first town he came upon was the seacoast town of Azotus. Once more the power of the Gospel was unleashed. How many believed in Christ, and whether Phillip stayed in that city for a week or a year, we do not know.

Upon leaving Azotus this young man turned north again, still following the beaches of the Mediterranean Sea. Whenever he came to a town he stopped. He preached the Gospel. He kept this up, city after city, until finally he came to Caesarea. This may have taken him only a few months; it is more likely it took quite a long time. Perhaps several years! His stay in each town was probably dictated by whether or not a church was already there when he arrived and how many Jerusalem believers were there. It probably took Phillip a considerable time to get to Caesarea, the Roman capital of Judea.

It was in Caesarea that Phillip paused.

Now let's go back for a moment. Earlier it was pointed out that Phillip was "unique in history." How was he unique? He not only signaled the beginning of that second group of men, he not only proclaimed the Gospel in cities throughout Judea, he is the first man in church history to ever receive a *gift.*

In Jerusalem there had been two groups of people: the Apostles and the believers. There had never been any other group. Then, eight years after Pentecost, something new happened. *Phillip happened!* (Remember, though, it took eight years . . . and this first gift had come about in the incomparable church in Jerusalem with twelve Apostles present, no less.) By the divine selection of the Holy Spirit, Phillip introduced something new into church history. There were no longer just Apostles; a second gift was added; there was now a man on earth functioning as something called "an evangelist." This is a wholly new term with a wholly new kind of man to fit it.

An evangelist is *not* an Apostle. Until Phillip such a thing had never been seen. Church history was nearly nine years old before church life produced the first "gifted" man . . . and his gift was *evangelism!* God gave something new to the church in Phillip. But God did *not* give His gift to the church, or to Phillip, until Phillip had gone through years of incredible preparation. (Gifted men should never come into being any other way.)

The church suddenly had a new dimension. Until now the raising up of a church was something done by Apostles. They began the church. They raised it. Now, along came Phillip. Please note he did not incorporate as a non-profit, tax-exempt corporation, buy a circus tent and launch an independent ministry. That will have to wait 1,800 more years. No, Phillip *aided* the Apostles. He worked with them for building a locatable, attendable church. One in every city. He was not carrying on an independent ministry. He had spent eight years at the feet of the very men he now helped; and he had spent just as many years in church life as a simple brother. Please note that Phillip gave his life to the church; he was an instrument in her hands to build her up, to make her glorious. The church was *not* a tool in his hand to be used to advance his ministry. All things were for the church.

Such is the way of a first century evangelist.

What is an evangelist? We really do not know. We will know what an evangelist *really* is when—once more upon this earth—true church life has produced one!

It had been a long, glorious saga for Phillip. Nothing of Saul's intention to destroy the church had been realized! Saul had succeeded only in introducing *another* Stephen! In fact, there would soon be even more "Stephens" and "Phillips" springing up all over the place.

That is the way it would go for the next four years. Wherever the disciples went they proclaimed Christ. If they stopped to live in a town, they began immediately to assemble in homes as the church.

For the next four years the twelve Apostles would keep abreast of all the young churches; they would visit some and strengthen others. Finally the Apostles were beginning to travel! Nonetheless, their activities were still confined to the tiny area of Judea.

Daily, the proclaiming of Christ intensified. Of approximately 200 villages, towns, and cities within the Judean territory, most of them were implanted with the church within four to five years after the death of Stephen. That is still a world's record for church expansion. Judea was completely evangelized! And all this time you thought those Apostles had been wasting their time! No, it is the twentieth century believer with his "the hour is late, we need a crash program, God is in a hurry to do a quick work this time" who is wasting his time.

Now you can see what eight years of a strong, mature, proper foundation in Jerusalem made possible. Yes, at first it really did look like nothing was happening. All twelve Apostles in one place, only one church on the whole planet . . . for eight years! It even looked like the Apostles were disobeying the Lord. (Fortunately they had no one from the twentieth century around to point this out!) Suddenly, at the end of nearly a decade, the flood gates burst! In the four years that followed there were easily over one hundred established churches in Judea. In addition to this, a number of empowered men also came forth.

Try topping *these* results by twentieth century methods.

In the coming years you will see a great deal of the Kingdom of God rest on the shoulders of this second group of men, this new breed. Just remember that all this took (1) time, (2) Apostles, (3) church life, and (4) living in the very depths of the experience of Jesus Christ.

And if you think that eight years seems like a terribly long time, just consider the 120. For the 3,000 it had been eight years of sitting. For the 120 it had been twelve years: eight in Jerusalem plus the nearly four years before that when they were following the Lord around!

And it was worth it all. It was glorious! A blazing witness to Christ now burned in almost every city in Judea.

Let's go visit some of those Judean churches and see what they look like!

18

Church Life, Judean Style

Church life in Judea! What was it like?

The answer is simple: it was exactly like church life in Jerusalem.

Even the beginning in Judea was similar to the beginning in Jerusalem. For instance, when the disciples arrived in Judea, they were jobless, homeless, and penniless. They had nothing, and they were in a strange place. But this was old hat for 3,000 of them. They had been jobless, homeless and broke before—right after Pentecost. Furthermore, they knew what to do in such a situation. They would solve this problem in 38 a.d. the same way they did in 30 a.d.

As church life was born in Jerusalem, so it was born in Judea.

As the believers began finding one another in the small towns throughout Judea, they undoubtedly got together, pooled what money and food they had, rented a house and piled in together. Other believers en route to other towns probably used the house for an overnight stopover, too. It was Jerusalem all over again.

Immediately those who were staying in a town started looking for ways to earn a living. The house where they lived automatically became the place for the church to assemble. None of this was hard to get used to; they had lived this way in Jerusalem for nearly a decade!

What about evangelism? *This* was different.

In evangelism Judea was very unlike Jerusalem! In Jerusalem, you will recall, the Apostles had a corner on this project. But in Judea, it was not twelve Apostles but hundreds of ordinary saints who proclaimed the Gospel! All the time these uprooted believers were finding one another, pooling their money, renting a house and moving in together, they were *also* blistering the city with the Gospel of salvation. Local citizens were being saved in the market place, and curious residents were coming over to the meetings. It was quite an hour.

Men today talk about the power of Pentecost and, as they tell the tale, they invariably ascribe great deeds and incredible power to the 3,000, saying "They shook Jerusalem and the whole world!" In fact, however, it was only the twelve who deserve such laurels. (*They* shook Jerusalem.) Men who say *all 3,000* were empowered at Pentecost are exactly eight years off in their calculations! It was in Judea that hundreds began to witness. Mark this: it was a decade after Pentecost before those who were saved on the day of Pentecost began to exercise the *power* of Pentecost. And that is the way it is supposed to be!

Remember, *these* are the people who were present at the *real* Pentecost. *They* are the example we should watch to find out what Pentecost really does to people.

There was another difference in evangelism in Judea. You recall that in Jerusalem the Lord used miracles and other incredible happenings to bring so many people to salvation. But these things were not so evident in Judea. In Judea there was just an awful lot of powerful witnessing and a whole lot of church life.

Every time God does a new work He introduces something fresh in it. Judea was God's new work, and the one new thing He introduced was the huge number of people who went out bearing witness to Christ.

Why hadn't this same thing happened before in Jerusalem? Why hadn't there been hundreds of people out evangelizing there, too? Because when God faced *the crisis* of the birth of the church, He could find only twelve men trained, trustable, broken and qualified to carry on the work of raising up the church. It was those men and those alone whom He used. Eight years later, when He faced *the crisis* of the dispersion, the number of qualified vessels He found available had increased somewhat! So He empowered them.

So the Judean churches were like Jerusalem in life style, but somewhat different in the way they evangelized.

What about the meetings?

The meetings of the churches in Judea were almost *exactly* like the meetings in Jerusalem.

Don't misunderstand. Those meetings must have been glorious: probably half of the room was filled with saints from Jerusalem, rejoicing at what God had done in bringing so many new people to Himself; and the other half was packed with wide-eyed new converts rejoicing in their salvation.

Nonetheless, the meetings were a duplicate of Jerusalem.

Why?

Because the transplanted believers were *all* from Jerusalem. Because they were all Jews. Because they had no other concept of church life and no other way of meeting except what they had experienced in Jerusalem. This was a danger signal, however. A serious one.

God's first way of expanding the church was by *transplanting* it. It was a way thought up by God and ordained by God; nonetheless, it proved to have one weakness: sameness. There is danger when all churches have such total uniformity. For this reason, at this very same time, God was laying plans for another great work, a new work in another nation, among pagans, *far* away from Judea. In that new place God would introduce infinite variety to His church.

But before we leave those home meetings in Judea, let's take just a little closer look at them. These meetings, after all, were really quite remarkable. Why? Because they had *no* leaders. No one was in charge. These home meetings were not directed by men!

But weren't there prophets and teachers to speak, to instruct? Absolutely not. God had not yet even given prophets and teachers to the church. Such things did not yet exist on this earth.

A church must never have its beginning with a whole lot of prophets and teachers present. That would ruin everything! The healthiest experience a church can have is to be born having at least some meetings that are utterly leaderless. The church, any church, has a *right* to such a joyous, dangerous, hair-raising experience! Such meetings build a strong foundation in the church and provide a counterbalance for the day when prophets and teachers *are* raised up. When that day arrives, the church will not be dependent on such men, nor will the meetings be centered around them. They will only be one more added ingredient, not the cornerstone that holds the meeting together.*

Then weren't there elders? No, God had not yet invented elders either.

What about Apostles? The Apostles were still in hiding in Jerusalem. When they did get out of town and into Judea, their visits were only intermittent and brief.

Who was in charge, then?

No one.

Then wasn't there chaos?

No.

Then was this "the spontaneous church" men speak of today?

No. There is no such thing as a spontaneous church—at least *not one that ever survives!*

Then without prophets, teachers, elders, or Apostles, what kept them from falling apart? What kept them afloat and on course? After all, those people were still experiencing at least some degree of persecution from the religious world. They were under pressure. If they were leaderless, where did they get their direction and stability? What was their secret?

Their secret was that they had already had eight long years of church life before they ever came to Judea.

If a new church has a number of people with this kind of *genuine* church experience, then you can be sure there will be some measure of true depth, brokenness, forbearance, patience, love and oneness among those people. A body of people who *have previously experienced church life* can survive, flourish and advance for a pretty good length of time with absolutely no help. They need no offices, no gifts and

---

*Don't get the idea, though, that home meetings without leaders are easy to come by. They are virtually impossible to have; but they *can* happen when the church has been properly founded.

no leaders. They can be, should be, just ordinary people who have had a long period of previous church experience. The foundation that has been laid in them will hold *without any structure whatsoever!*

Every church needs a period when it has no leaders. It is always one of her most beautiful times. The corporateness, oneness, and love during such a period is a fragrance to God and man. In fact, it is this period of time, while the church is giftless and leaderless, which God uses to begin to raise up gifted men. But it must have a strong foundation in order to survive this period.

One last thing about the meetings in Judea.

They were a pure expression of the Hebrew heart. This is very important. Those meetings were Hebrew meetings; they fit Hebrews!

What does this mean? Is this important?

Let's say you had been an unbelieving Jew in those days. One day you decided to attend a meeting of this thing called the church which had recently hit your town. What would your impression be of one of those meetings? You would definitely have beheld something unlike anything else you had ever seen before in your whole life! And yet, at the same time, you would have felt right at home. You would not have seen anything that looked foreign. You would have seen joyous Hebrews being Hebrews. They would have been expressing Christ in their own natural, native way.

The church fits its environment. The church *matches* the people and the nation in which it grows.

Now please note this fact: this beautiful thing, that is, the church matching the nation it was in, would not have happened if the twelve Apostles had been foreigners. (God does not *always* use the Jerusalem line. As you will see later, God does not use this way when the Apostles are *not* native to the land.)

Here, then, is an important lesson: Apostles must not stay a long time in one place (the Jerusalem way) if those Apostles are *foreigners* in that place. If they do, it will be disastrous, especially should the church they raise up later engage in transplanting itself into other cities and nations.

This can be illustrated.

Let's say the twelve Apostles had all been born in Japan. Let's say that one day they all moved to London, England where they raised up a great testimony of the church. Imagine that these Englishmen sat at the feet of the twelve Apostles for eight years. Then one day, everyone in the church in London got up, left London, and dispersed all over the British Isles. Imagine the London church replanted in Sussex, Wales, Scotland and maybe even Ireland. Now what would that transplanted church look like to a Scotsman or a Welshman?

Would the church really look English? Would it fit England? Could Englishmen easily identify with it? Or would it look Japanese?

The fact is, the meetings would not look English and they would not look Japanese. Neither an Englishman *nor* a Japanese would feel comfortable in that expression of the church. People who were originally in the church in London, sitting under the twelve (Japanese) Apostles every day, may have loved it. They may never have even noticed that they were gradually becoming very peculiar Englishmen themselves, because of the Japanese influence they were under. But you can be sure of this: if that church were *transplanted* throughout the rest of Britain, it would definitely look odd to everyone else! What would the Japanese-influenced English meetings look like then?

Peculiar. That's all. Just peculiar!

Why? Because it would be too much a blend of that which is Japanese and that which is English and, especially, that which is *neither.* The Japanese Apostles could not be fully Japanese; and the young English believers would not be truly English, because of their inevitable imitation of the Apostles' ways. In fact, that London church would not really fit anywhere. Such an oddity cannot be prevented if the Apostles are foreign to the land in which they are working, and if they reside with the original church *for a long period of time.*

Furthermore, if that church in London were transplanted to the Continent, it would look even more peculiar there! At least in Britain it would have had a few identifiable British traits. But in Italy, for example, the transplanted church would look incredibly strange to a local Italian.

Go back and look at the Jerusalem church. What was its composition? The people who made up the church in Jerusalem had come from three sources: (1) Jews who had been saved in Jerusalem but who came from other parts of the Roman Empire; (2) those who were Jerusalem citizens, thousands of whom were saved during the eight years; and (3) people from Judea who moved into Jerusalem to be part of the world's only church! Perfect! Just what God wanted.

And what about the Apostles? Where were they from? Every one of them, to the man, was born and raised within *thirty miles* of Jerusalem! They were all local, all native.

Here is the point.

God gave the *Jerusalem line* as a very *specialized* way of raising up the church. In the Jerusalem line, God began with only one church, the Jerusalem church. This was literally the only church on earth for eight years. This is as it should be, for God always takes His time when He establishes a *beginning work*. The foundation is not quickly laid.

God gave the Jerusalem line for beginnings. He gave it to Apostles native to the area. He gave the Jerusalem line for transplanting the church . . . but transplanting it only in the area of its birth.

A beginning takes time, lots of time, in one place. And in the Jerusalem line, the Apostles are a very dominant factor; therefore, they *must* be from the local area, or the church turns out peculiar, not fitting the nation it is in.

The Jerusalem line was a special work of God; God used it for a beginning work, for Apostles native to the country, and for transplanting.

In summary we see that the churches transplanted from Jerusalem, into Judea, *fit* Judea. The *original* church had been raised up by twelve local Jews; this church was part of the nation into which it went. If the twelve Apostles had come from, say India, to raise up the Jerusalem church, and if, at the end of eight years, that church had been transplanted throughout Judea, then the new churches would not have fit Judea.

Why bring up this point?

Because all the history of missionaries' methods is a violation of the basic principles God used to raise up the church! This is but *one* example of that fact.

In Jerusalem we see the *first way God gave* for the raising up of His church; in Judea, we see the second way He used.

So far, then, God has given two basic ways of raising up His church. Both ways are part of what we call the Jerusalem line.

THE JERUSALEM LINE—God's first great work—looks something like this:
1. The *first* way to raise up the church: *Jerusalem*
    A. Jerusalem was a genesis church.
    B. Twelve Apostles were present. Apostles were needed because Jerusalem was a beginning work.
    C. And because it was a beginning, it took *time.*
    D. Because this church would later be planted in other cities, the Apostles were *local.*
2. The *second* way God gave to raise up the church: *Judea.*
    A. The Jerusalem church was now planted in Judea, the country of its birth.
    B. The ordinary believers, not the Apostles, were the key to raising up those churches. Apostles were not needed because of the strong foundation in the lives of the believers . . . a foundation they received in Jerusalem.
    C. The "transplanting" way of raising up the church was confined almost solely to the culture of the people involved.

So much for the life style, the evangelism and the meetings of the churches in Judea. Let us go on; there are a few other things the Judean churches have to teach us.

Number one. In Judea the unity of the church was kept. There never was but one church in the city of Jerusalem. But that was Jerusalem! *Now,* the church has reached Judea! What will the believers do once they get free of the Apostles? Here is a golden opportunity for them to do things the way *they* want. Here is the opportunity to settle grudges, grind theological axes, draw doctrinal lines and, most of all, to pursue special interests. ("We never have given enough time to winning lepers to Christ!") What a chance to launch a raft

140

of "interdenominational organizations." Most of all, here is the big chance to launch a dozen different churches in every city.

Did they?

They did *not!*

In every city of Judea there was still unity—visibly depicted. There was still one church per city.

Was this because absolutely everyone adhered to one all-inclusive, iron clad *doctrinal view*? Did everyone believe *exactly* the same thing? Was *that* the secret of the unity of the early church? Impossible. If there had been a *demand* for total unity of believers, there would have been at least a dozen churches per city. A demand for everyone to believe exactly the same way is what causes disunity.

No, it was not an enforced doctrinal agreement that produced this unity. Far from it.

Was it organization that held them together, one great superstructure, with ecumenical headquarters in Jerusalem? No. It was not a monolithic organizational structure that was their secret.

There was unity in the Judean churches partly because no one had ever gotten around to inventing doctrinal statements. And the early church *never* got organized. Not locally, and not Roman Empire-wide! The main reason for the unity of the believers was that they were enamored with Jesus Christ. They were overwhelmed with the daily experience of encountering Jesus Christ. He alone possessed them. *He* was their unity.

Unity will never be known any other way.

Just look at the believers as they entered Judea.

They showed a total lack of twentieth century imagination. No variety. No "church on every street corner." No independent ministries. No specialized organizations for specific groups of people. No seminaries founded to train and harness the wealth of fresh, young talent. Just the church, the whole church, and nothing but the church. How unimaginative can you get?

There was true, practical, visible unity in the early church.

141

Number two. The dispersion into Judea spotlighted the mobility and abandonment of the followers of Christ.

You recall that the Jerusalem church had been born in mobility—thousands of people left their homes in other parts of the Empire in order to deliberately settle in a place new to them. This meant a leap of faith into the unknown. A blind trust in the future prospect of the Kingdom of God. Out of this leap came total abandonment, a deliberate loss of absolutely everything. That was the standard set in Jerusalem!

The standard of abandonment, first raised in Jerusalem, was now carried to new heights in Judea.

In one night those same Jerusalem believers left everything again and blazed into Judea. They moved out of Jerusalem into Judea with *nothing,* just as they had once moved into Jerusalem with nothing! They had only their bare hands by which they could earn a living, and with that *alone* they rebuilt their lives and put a church in every city in that nation! What a people! What an hour!

And every bit of it was done, not in remorse, but in the midst of great joy!

May God have such a people again on this earth.

Number three. Judea did point up two or three danger signals. The first danger signal, the sameness of all the churches, has already been pointed out. Fortunately, this conformity was not deliberate. In our age men purposely launch movements which, as they spread, are *intended* to be identical. Such a practice, of course, is an abomination to God.

God never planned for all the churches on earth to be so much alike, and yet to date, all were alike! But God would remedy this situation by launching a *new* work which would produce a second strain of churches. Without exception, these churches would each be different from the others—radically so. This new line of churches would serve as a balance to what happened in Judea.

(The day will come, later in the century, when *all* these churches, those in the Jerusalem line, and in the Antioch line, will honor one another. All will hold to the sanctity of the unity of the body in each city.)

We spot a *second* danger signal in Judea.

If you had been there you could easily have identified the problem: the Jews simply did not think in terms of salvation for anyone but Jews. No one else was even welcome unless, of course, he had been fully proselytized to Judaism.

Evangelism in Judea had been breathtaking, but it had also been racially exclusive. Just look! There were between 100 and 200 towns in Judea, Galilee and the surrounding Jewish areas. How long did the evangelization of Judea take? How long for 20,000 people to raise up the church, say in 150 towns?

Four years!

Pretty good for a people who went nowhere during their first eight years of church life.

But if you had asked a believer how much *more* evangelizing needed to be done, his answer might have surprised you: "Well, there is a church in virtually every town in Judea, Galilee and Samaria. There are believers and a church in Damascus and other parts of Syria. Well, that covers about 4/5 of the Jews in Palestine, so our job is almost over. Of course there are large numbers of Jews in Rome, Italy and Alexandria, Egypt and some other big cities. I suspect the Apostles may get to those cities someday and tell the rest of our people about Christ. But all in all I would say the bigger part of the task is over."

Absolutely no one was thinking of taking the Gospel to *anyone* but Jews. The idea of going to non-Jews, the idea of *evangelizing the world,* was just as remote as the idea of taking the Gospel to cats and parakeets would be in our day. It simply never entered the minds of those believers that anyone except Jews was supposed to hear the Gospel.

The Jews literally did not realize God intended salvation for all mankind. But He did; and He was very determined to break through the confines of Judaism.

There was a *third* danger signal. The Judean churches were beginning to move back into the traditions of the Jewish faith. Some of the ancient Jewish religious customs were still being practiced by the disciples—customs that *should* have been dropped.

143

For instance, once the believers settled in a Judean town, they immediately joined the local synagogue! It is very likely that attendance at those synagogues actually shot up with the influx of the believers into Judea! Not only that, the followers of Christ actually took up jobs in those synagogues. They became ushers, for example, and carried on the custom of letting wealthy people sit near the front and telling the poor to sit on the floor.

No wonder God was restless.

God wanted His church to break free of all such religious practices and, specifically, from Jewish legalism. But in a land that dripped with religious custom, whose very atmosphere was scented with ritual, and where Judaism literally flowed in a man's bloodstream, God could not possibly get that *total* break.

There was a way, however, and there was a place; and God was making His plans.

Let's take one last look at Judea. The dispersion began in 38 a.d. By 41 a.d. most of the 20,000 had settled down somewhere. Just how far had the Gospel and the church reached some eleven years after Pentecost? Not far!

The church had spread into Judea, Galilee, and Samaria to such cities as Azotus, Joppa, Lydda, and Caesarea. That was about a sixty mile perimeter! A few disciples had actually touched some other nations beyond that. They had reached the country of Syria, establishing the church in Damascus. That covers a circle of about 125 miles.

A handful of disciples had gone beyond this 125 mile limit. They had gone as far as the Isle of Cyprus, 200 miles north. Remember, almost all of this took place between 38 and 41 a.d.

The *most distant point* reached was a city in Syria called Antioch, 300 miles north of Jerusalem. Antioch was the very last city which the dispersion had touched, and probably no more than a dozen people got that far.

Let's sum up. In the first eight years of church history, there was one church on this earth and only twelve Apostles, all in one town. In the next four years over 150 churches were born! So the tally changed to about 150 churches, twelve Apostles, one evangelist, plus a lot of other believers who had suddenly taken on new and heavy responsibilities.

By all modern day standards of Christianity with its "crash program" and "time is short" mentality, these people were real laggers. (Only 125 miles?) Except for that energetic little bunch of men who hit Antioch, the spread of the Gospel and the spread of the church had pretty well come to an end. Nonetheless, admit it; it was an incredible record. It has never been topped in all modern history. The modern day believer has much to learn, and nothing to teach, compared with their example.

The church, the churches, looked glorious. There were a few danger signals. The Lord still wanted to move higher. And move He was about to do!

How?

To answer that question we have to return to the days right after Stephen's death, and see what was happening at that time in Jerusalem. From there we will be able to trace the birth of God's second great work upon the earth.

19

The Jerusalem Church Reborn

Saul was infuriated.

In one night the whole city had emptied of believers. It was incomprehensible! How could 20,000 people just up and disappear? Normal people don't just leave their houses, possessions and jobs at a moment's notice.

But these weren't ordinary people. They had no attachment to anything material. Yes, they had gone in the blink of an eye.

At first Saul, and the Sanhedrin, probably surmised this sudden disappearance meant the end of "the Way." They could not have guessed the durability and elasticity of these people. But Saul's hopes were shattered when he heard that these ex-Jerusalem citizens were pouring into Damascus, Syria in record numbers. Saul probably got the impression based on first reports, that Damascus might end up hosting a transplant of the whole Jerusalem church! He was not clear exactly what was happening in Damascus; he was only sure of one thing: he wanted to go to Damascus and eliminate any possibility of the church getting a foothold there. (Saul seemed not to be aware of the staggering events taking place out there in the little towns of Judea.)

Saul went to the Sanhedrin.

His work in Jerusalem was complete. He wanted legal permission to go to Damascus and crush the heretics there even before they got started. It was obvious that Saul planned to dedicate his whole life to destroying the body of Christ.

He received permission.

What he actually ended up with was sort of a hunting license for any Jewish believers anywhere within the religious jurisdiction of the Sanhedrin. With legal documents in hand Saul gathered up his best associates and set out for Damascus. He probably went by horse and may even have had a small militia along with him. One thing is sure, with every breath he was breathing vengeance on the church.

At this point, just a few days after Stephen's death, the outlook for the future of the church was grave. As long as Saul was around there was little hope the believers could survive. The outlook for the saints who had fled to Damascus was black indeed.

Oddly enough, Saul never got to Damascus. Or, if he did, he never did anything. It was almost as if he disappeared off the earth. The Sanhedrin never even got a report back from him.

Judaism had somehow lost its chief persecutor. The driving force behind this holocaust had vanished. The Sanhedrin did not seem to mind too much. Their main objective had been reached. The church had been stamped out in Jerusalem. *That* was the main thing.

In a year or two the whole idea of destroying the church had lost its momentum. The church was no longer a major threat to the existence of the Sanhedrin. They could learn to live with scattered pockets of believers here and there.

Persecution definitely died down after Saul's mysterious disappearance, but it did not completely cease. How long, exactly, did the persecution last? It appears the church lived under rather mild, intermittent harassment for another three years.

How long was Jerusalem without an expression of the church?

It appears that about the third or fourth year after Stephen's death a few saints began trickling back into the Holy City. Probably a few quiet meetings even began to be held in homes. Everyone was cautious, but it appeared the church might make a small comeback in the face of a secure, disinterested Sanhedrin.

We do not know who returned, how many returned, when they returned, or even why they returned, but we do

148

know that little by little the church in Jerusalem was coming back into existence . . . even if it had to go underground to do so.

We know the name of only one person who returned to Jerusalem. Barnabas returned.

It was about 41 a.d. The church was getting back on its feet. Suddenly, though, Barnabas heard some very bad news.

20

The Unlikeliest Convert

Word shot through the city.

"Saul is back in town."

The man who had tried to destroy the church three years earlier had come back to Jerusalem. Had he returned to lay siege to the church again? No one knew! The last time anyone had seen Saul was when he left for Damascus in 38 a.d. It was not really clear in anyone's mind just exactly what had happened to him after that, nor what was his attitude, now in the year 41 a.d., toward the church.

A rumor had gone around that he had been converted to Christ. But it was *only* a rumor. The fact was no one knew anything for certain. Was he Saul the persecutor, or Saul a fellow heir of Christ?

(Saul, by our reckoning, is about thirty-two now.)

One of the men who heard the news of Saul's return was Joseph-Barnabas. Something within Barnabas believed the rumor about Saul's conversion. He also heard that Saul had come to Jerusalem hoping to see Peter. Barnabas set out to locate Saul. When the two men stood face to face for the first time, it marked the first encounter between two men who would one day alter the course of human history!

Saul and Barnabas talked extensively. Barnabas listened. Saul told his experiences of the past few years. It was crystal clear. There could be no mistake: Saul *was* a believer. He had the life of Christ! Amazing!

With that point cleared up, Barnabas escorted Saul to Peter's dwelling . . . probably his hiding place. There in that room Simon Peter (and James) met one Saul of Tarsus. They too were treated to the story of Saul's spectacular conversion. Barnabas told them how Saul had boldly proclaimed Christ to the Jews in Damascus right after his conversion.

Peter listened, then he invited Saul to stay with him for as long as he remained in Jerusalem. The two men talked a long time, a very long time. In fact Saul lived with Peter for two weeks. It must have been quite an experience for both men.

That day Saul probably never guessed he would shortly need a hiding place himself. Saul never got to attend a meeting of the church or meet anyone else there.

What happened?

Visiting with Peter was only one of two things Saul wanted to do during his stay in Jerusalem. Saul had an old debt to pay while in town. There were some Greek-speaking Jews in the city he wished to speak to.

Saul strolled over to the Libertine synagogue.

The very walls of the building must have cried out to him as he recalled a scene which took place there. He knew what he had to do. He quickly challenged those present to a debate, on the very spot where he had once faced Stephen! (Barnabas was almost certainly there to see the whole thing.) Saul against the local Jews, on the subject of Jesus Christ! Barnabas was undoubtedly overwhelmed with what he saw. He never forgot that day.

It was a spectacular turn-around: Saul recreating a scene almost identical to the one which had taken place on the same spot three years earlier. Remember? Stephen had debated these very same men. He had thoroughly trounced them all, including Saul! Saul remembered! He also recalled that during that same season they had murdered Stephen. Now he stood up. He had never known Stephen as a believer, or as a friend. But today he sought, in some small way, to pay a debt to a man he wished he *had* known and had listened to. Saul let loose with all he had. Under the anointing of God he must have wilted his opponents in their tracks. They must have been stunned. Instead of opposing Stephen's view, Saul was proclaiming it! Saul boldly declared that Jesus Christ was truly Israel's Messiah! His former colleagues were not prepared for this, nor did they intend to accept it.

Saul's words came very close to producing the same results that Stephen's had. The Jews were furious. The idea of *Saul* being a convert to "the way!" Soon after the debate, a murderous plot was once more concocted—this time *against Saul!*

Fortunately the outcome of this plot would be different from the one hatched against Stephen.

Disciples in the city got wind of the pending assassination. (This is why Saul never got to go to a meeting of the church! He probably had to spend his two weeks in Jerusalem in Peter's hide-a-way.) Immediately they made plans to smuggle Saul safely out of Jerusalem. What a reversal! The man who had persecuted the church was now being persecuted *for* it. Those whom Saul once sought to destroy were now saving *him* from destruction. The disciples finally managed to sneak Saul out of the city and up the coast to the seaport city of Caesarea. (Saul could never have imagined that someday he would spend two years in prison in this very city that now gave him flight.) There at the docks they saw him off on a boat set to sail northward to Tarsus, Celicia.

Saul was on a 300 mile trip back to his home town.

It had been a short stay in Jerusalem. He had been with Peter exactly fifteen days. He had not met the other Apostles. Neither the church nor any of the believers had so much as seen his face. Nonetheless, everyone heard the news. Saul, the persecutor, had received the Lord. Everyone rejoiced at the incredible news.

Saul was about twenty-nine years old when converted in 38 a.d. He disappeared for three years, emerging for two weeks in about 41 a.d. and now he vanishes again. We will not hear of him for three more years.

It was at this time (41 a.d.) that all persecution finally subsided in Jerusalem and Judea.

At last peace began to settle in on Judea. The churches of Judea, Samaria and Galilee found rest from affliction. Even in Jerusalem it appears that the church knew a respite from danger. So, with rest from fear of man and with a Godly fear of the Lord and by the comfort the Lord Himself had given them, the churches grew and multiplied.

About eleven years have passed since Pentecost. The Emperor Gaius Caligula (37-41) has just died. Claudius has taken his place. And God is laying the foundation for His second great work, a work that equals even Pentecost in its importance.

Let's see the first small beginnings of that work..

21

Look Who Came To Dinner

Peter packed a few things, said good-by to his wife, and slipped out of Jerusalem.

He was off on one of those "Apostle visits" to a new church. This time he was headed for the church in Lydda, twenty-four miles west of Jerusalem. He did not know, no one knew, that by the time he returned home church history would have started into one of its most important turns. It would be many years before anyone would realize the far-reaching significance of this little trip.

Soon after Peter's arrival in Lydda, two believers from the seaport city of Joppa arrived. They had come to Peter bearing some very sad news. It seems one of the most beloved women in the church in Joppa had just died. Her name was Tabitha (or, by interpretation, Dorcas). Because the churches throughout Judea were still very young, the death of a believer was a rarity. Not many churches had gone through this experience. Having explained the reason for their coming, the two men then asked Peter to please come up to Joppa with them. Peter agreed. What they had in mind, what he had in mind, is not known. The three men set out together to make the eleven mile trek to the Mediterranean Sea.

Upon arriving in Joppa, Peter went straight to the room where Dorcas' body was being kept. Walking in, he asked everyone else to leave the room; he knelt down beside the body, and then addressed the corpse: "Tabitha, arise."

And arise she did!

Of course when news of *this* got out it caused no small stir in the city. After all, a dead person had been raised. Many

155

believed in the Lord as a result, and Peter decided to stay in Joppa for a while.*

Further north, in the city of Caesarea, something else new was happening. A man by the name of Cornelius, a non-Jew who was a captain in the Italian army, was in his home praying. He was a very pious, God-fearing man! While he was offering his regular 3 o'clock-in-the-afternoon prayers, something unusual happened: an angel appeared to him in a vision. The angel told Cornelius to send three men to Joppa to get a man named Peter and to bring him back with them to Caesarea.

Peter, in the meantime, (still in the city of Joppa) also had a very remarkable experience of his own. He had gone up on the roof of the home where he was staying (sort of a roof garden) at about noon with the intention of praying. While there, he received a very clear and very startling vision from the Lord. The essense of this particular vision was this: even *non-Jews* could receive the Lord Jesus as Savior!

Now that was a very, very revolutionary idea.

The vision ended. Peter just sat there for a while pondering the full implication of what he had been shown. The Spirit of the Lord then spoke to him: "There are three men looking for you. Go with them."

Peter went downstairs and, sure enough, three men were standing at the front gate of the house. Peter invited them in, then asked them to stay for supper and to spend the night. They were gentiles! From Caesarea. They wanted Peter to go to Caesarea with them. In fact, they had actually come to fetch him. The next day the four of them, along with some other Jewish believers, left for Caesarea. Peter was making his second unscheduled visit on this trip.

Where were they going? To the home of a man named Cornelius.

*For the record, this was the first time an Apostle had raised the dead. Please note it has been at least eleven years since Pentecost, years of maturing and experience in Peter *and* in the church . . . . . Yes, Peter had been an Apostle for a decade before he raised the dead! Let the record show that it was *at least* ten years after Pentecost before God had a man who could raise the dead! (So don't be too quick to demand some earth shaking sign from an Apostle, should you ever happen upon one . . . . which isn't likely. Even Peter couldn't meet all "the standards" . . . . yet he was an Apostle.)

When Peter reached Cornelius' home, the two men exchanged their astonishing stories. Cornelius explained that he was so certain Peter would come that he had even calculated Peter's time of arrival, and had invited his friends over to meet Peter. Cornelius then conducted Peter into another room where, much to his astonishment, Peter found himself face to face with a room full of gentiles! They were all sitting there eagerly waiting to hear about the Lord Jesus Christ.

As Peter looked over the room, he finally began to grasp what was going on. God *was* opening the Gospel to non-Jews, just as God had revealed to him in the vision! The despised gentiles were going to get a chance to know Christ!

This was historic!

Peter stood right there in front of them and admitted it was unlawful for him to be in the same room with them, and, furthermore, this was the first time in his life he had ever encountered a group of gentiles. Undaunted, Peter began to address them.

But before his message was completed, something amazing happened: the Holy Spirit fell upon his uncircumcised listeners. It was a rerun of Pentecost! The difference was that this time it was gentiles! Everyone received the Holy Spirit, spoke in tongues, and exalted the true and living God.

It was three o'clock in the afternoon. The year 41 a.d.

It was a very significant day. For the first time in all history gentiles were taken out and baptized in the name of Jesus Christ. Peter! Baptizing gentiles! Now that was something.

When news of this got back to Jerusalem it caused quite a stir. Sure enough, when Peter returned home he was in hot water. Even with some of the Apostles. What was the problem? They were upset because Peter had eaten a meal with gentiles! (So, you see, the Jerusalem church did have quite a little problem with provincial prejudice and Scriptural legalism.)

Peter well understood their confusion. He didn't even think their being upset was unusual! Then he unraveled the whole amazing story. Immediately their attitudes changed, and they praised God for what had happened in Caesarea.

Still, somehow, everyone seemed to have overlooked the main question: should these new converts be circumcised before they went on with Christ—thereby making them Jews? At that moment no one dreamed such a daring question even existed. In upcoming years circumcision would become one of the biggest issues of the church, but not now. (So what happened to Cornelius? Did he, and the other gentiles get circumcised? Well, dear reader, unbelievable as it may seem, this first group of gentiles were almost surely circumcised and made proselyte Jews. Otherwise they would not have been allowed to fellowship in the church in Caesarea!)

Joseph-Barnabas must have been one of the brothers who heard Peter tell the incredible story of the gentiles' conversion. As he listened, something deep inside him must have been stirred. In some way, a way that has never been told us, Barnabas must have been disturbed by the attitude of believers—the attitude that the gentiles *had* to first be made Jews in order to become followers of Christ.

The Lord, too, must have been troubled. The Gospel being preached in Jerusalem and Judea was a very provincial and exclusive Gospel. The churches simply did not know the extent of the riches of the grace of God toward anyone who believed. But the Lord had begun, a decade after Pentecost, to take steps to change those limitations of *His* Gospel.

Of course, what God had done in Jerusalem and Judea was great; it was His greatest work in all Hebrew history! But it was *not* the end of what He had planned. There were too many restrictions still holding back the freedom of His Gospel. The Lord was about to make a great leap in purifying His work even more. What was God about to do? God used this conversion of Cornelius, this *second* Pentecost, to launch His new work.

Where?

God had just moved! The Lord's main work from now on would be 300 miles *north* of Judea. A wholly new chapter of church history was about to be written. The first conversion of gentiles in Caesarea was only a first small step of something much more far-reaching. It was a crack in the door. The whole gatepost was about to fall!

You might say that one half of Pentecost took place in Jerusalem in May of 30 a.d. At that time half of the body (the Jew) was baptized into Christ. As a result of Pentecost, the Jews in Jerusalem heard the Gospel and the church was established in all the towns of Judea. This had taken over a decade. Then, in Cornelius' home the other half of Pentecost was completed, and the gentile was baptized into the body of Christ. The doors of the Gospel were finally cracked open, outwardly, from Judea.

The Gospel was about to break the bounds of one race and one nation. It was also about to break completely free of the religious system. Because of this *second* Pentecost, (actually the *completion* of Pentecost), the Lord was flinging open the gates for all nations to hear the Gospel *and* to experience the church.

We have now seen the genesis of a major turn in human history. Now let's take a trip up to the city of Antioch: God is about to do an amazing thing in that far away city.

22

Gentiles Unlimited

There it was, all spread out before them. It was the third largest city in the world.

The population: 500,000. Location, far from Jerusalem and Judea. Make up, Greek!

As they crossed the Syrian plateau, the exiles from Jerusalem could see the Orontes River flowing into Antioch and then winding downward through fifteen miles of hill country toward the Mediterranean Sea. Bordering the city on the south was Mt. Silpius. At the base of this mountain the disciples could clearly see a huge rock carving of a faceless human head. According to pagan myth, this was Charon, he who transported dead souls to the underworld. Five miles south of Antioch was the Grove of Daphne where, in the shadow of a huge statue of Apollo, immorality was disguised as religious ritual. In this same area was a forest which had become a sanctuary for criminals, debtors and escaped slaves.

As the little band of disciples moved closer to the city, they came out of the plateau onto a narrow, fertile plain. It was obvious Antioch was a beautiful example of city planning. Built fully in the tradition of Greco-Roman civilization, it was a "modern" city of that day. It was one of the most beautiful cities in the Empire. It was even called "Antioch the Beautiful" and "The Queen of the East."

The disciples entered the city on a broad, columned thoroughfare. They walked past the Inspired Legate, pagan temples, and the spectacular Hippodrome, antiquity's version of a race track. Of course, hidden from the beautiful center of the city, as in all such cities of that day, were miles of over-crowded back streets.

There was one thing different about this city. In all the other cities to which the brothers from Jerusalem had fled there were concentrated areas of Jewish populations and cultures. But Antioch was further from Jerusalem than any other place to which the persecuted believers had scattered. It was isolated, the only large city in the area. Yes, there were Jews here. Yes, there was a synagogue here, the second most beautiful synagogue on earth. And yes, the brothers would enter this synagogue and proclaim the Gospel. Nonetheless, Antioch was out and out gentile. Its language, culture and customs were a world away from Judean life.

Antioch could well have braced itself at the sight of these new-comers. Something revolutionary had hit town as that little band of men trooped through the gates. Neither the size of the city nor its distance from Judea was going to deter these saints. Although they were Jews, none of them had come from Jerusalem, not originally. They came from Cyrene in Northwest Africa and from the nearby island of Cyprus. Greek, not Hebrew, was their native tongue. Undoubtedly the whole lot of them had been in Jerusalem to observe Pentecost on that fateful day in May, 30 a.d. and had been converted under Peter's Gospel. Now, over a decade later, they were back in their own Greek-speaking world. They were right at home in Antioch.

How many men in this fleeing company of believers? Probably no more than eight to twelve.

This was no timid lot of men; their hearts were ablaze with Jesus Christ. And they were without racial qualms. They did something no one had ever done before, not in all Hebrew history. Once they opened fire with the Gospel, they indiscriminately proclaimed it to local Greeks just as they did to the Jews! They completely by-passed the custom of speaking only to the Jews at the local synagogue. Furthermore, the Greeks who heard them responded . . . with unbridled enthusiasm. Nowhere, ever, had there been a more immediate and open response to the message of Jesus Christ.

Suddenly the number of believers in Antioch ballooned. The brothers from Jerusalem were surrounded and almost enveloped by a great host of new "pagan believers." Scratching their heads they looked at their situation. They had a unique problem. Here were newly converted believers who had no Judeo-religious heritage. Words like "Abraham," "the chosen seed," "the line of David," "the convenant promise," "circumcision," "purification," and "Sabbath" were totally unknown concepts to them. No, these new gentile converts did not fit into the pattern of any previous believers. They were altogether ignorant of Hebrew life and history; they had no religious heritage; they had grown up totally outside the influence of a strong religious system. Their moral code was non-existent. They knew nothing of strict moral, social discipline. And they outnumbered the Jewish believers by a whopping percentage.

Apparently the outnumbered Jewish brothers could not stir up much interest in the topics of Hebrew tradition either. What the Greeks liked to hear about was the knowledge and experience of Jesus Christ. And those Jewish brothers, not being very learned in theological propriety, made a fatal mistake: they gave the gentiles only Christ . . . without all the other "trimmings."

In the days following, the number of believers grew even larger. With every day that passed, this crowd looked less and less Jewish and more and more like something no one had ever seen before. The Jewish brothers, it appears, finally threw in the towel completely. Things like circumcision, purification, etc. went out the window.

These were all very significant happenings, far too unusual to be totally overlooked even in far away Jerusalem. Word that so many pagans were following Christ was bound to reach the ears of the Apostles.

The Jerusalem believers were just beginning to get used to the idea of having gentile believers in the church in Caesarea, Judea. Now, suddenly, out of nowhere, came a report that a *host* of gentiles had turned to Christ in a far off city. In fact, if the report was to be believed, there were only a handful of *Jewish* believers in the entire group in Antioch. (And *that* bunch had proven the limits of their good judgment by witnessing to gentiles!)

Undoubtedly no one in the church in Jerusalem recognized the significance of this report. To a believer living in Judea, the story of gentiles coming to Christ was just one more amazing event in a long list of amazing things which God had been doing. There was no question, though, to the Judean believers that the main blessing of God was still with the Jews—it was certainly not with a handful of Greek converts in a distant gentile city.

They did not know God was changing the place of His *fullest* blessing. The main flow of God's work had moved to Antioch. And no one had even noticed! It would be years, perhaps decades, before this fact became evident to all.

Of course, the Jerusalem saints *did* realize that this new event in Antioch was wonderful. The news was a little strange, but they received it with great delight. They realized a story this wild, even if it did come from way up north in Antioch, was worth looking into.

Someone was needed to travel to Antioch, check out the situation, come back to Jerusalem and report what he saw to the Apostles. Antioch did *not* seem important enough to require a visit by an Apostle. After all, the Apostles were busy; they had their hands full in Judea. Still, whoever was chosen to go needed to be a solid brother and one who could speak Greek. The job was given to a reliable brother indeed, one known as the "son of encouragement." Barnabas got the job. The long trip was his. After thirteen years of sitting he was finally going to become part of the action.

It was a simple decision: an Apostle would not be needed. Barnabas could see what was happening in this "renegade" work of the Lord. The Apostles did not realize that they had greatly underestimated what was going on in Antioch. But it was a divine error.

God had decided, in the simple selection of Barnabas, to give him one of the key roles in determining the destiny of mankind for all time to come.

Everything about their decision was unique. For one thing, Barnabas was to be sent *alone*. Generally, when something like this was done, two men went. Furthermore, Barnabas was not sent to Antioch as an Apostle. He was *not* an Apostle; he went simply as a brother. (According to the terms used in the early churches, he was a "worker.") Barnabas' commission was simply to visit a city where there were some new believers. He was to report his findings. How long he was to stay, what he was supposed to do, when he was to return to Jerusalem, how he was to get the report back to the Apostles . . . all this seems to have been left up in the air.

Barnabas took his simple commission, bade everyone a warm goodbye, and slipped out of the city . . . alone.

It would be a long time before Barnabas returned to Jerusalem to give that report to the Apostles—probably a lot longer than anyone expected it to be. It would be even longer before the full meaning of what the Lord was doing in Antioch would be grasped by anyone.

(The day will even come when cataclysmic issues arise among the young churches. Barnabas will be at the very center of that controversy. In that day he will be on the opposite side of the fence from the very Apostles who are now sending him off to Antioch. Furthermore, it will be Barnabas, not the twelve, who will be standing in the Lord's greater light!)

Barnabas walked out of Jerusalem that day as a simple brother—a brother who had been in the church under the Apostles' instruction for about thirteen years. One day he will return to Jerusalem. When he does, he will not return as a brother only. No, on that day he will return as an Apostle in his own right.

Thirteen years have passed since Pentecost. Most of the Judean churches are five or six years old. There are about 150 churches, almost all of them are in a 125 mile area. Now, finally, a gentile church is about to be born.

Claudius is Emperor of Rome. Agrippa I is governor of Judea. The future destiny of western man is in the hands of Barnabas.

It is springtime. The year is 43 a.d.

23

The Second Work of God Begins

Gleefully they told Barnabas the story. Gentiles! Dozens of them. All believers. Greeks! In love with the Lord. "Barnabas, you have to see them. The meetings, too. Nothing is like it was back in Judea. Here in Antioch everything is different."

Like any other Jew, Barnabas must have been unnerved; he had never been in the same room with a crowd of gentiles. But if Peter could do it, so could Barnabas.

There was more to his attending this meeting than a willingness to break with the tradition of segregation: Barnabas had something on his heart. Antioch matched that burden. His conduct clearly shows he felt the Lord wanted an expression of the church which was a clear break with *all* past traditions. As Barnabas neared the meeting place he was going to have his chance to make that feeling a reality; but nothing in all his past had prepared him for what he was about to behold. He realized he probably was going to be shocked, getting a first glimpse of the gentile version of the Kingdom of God!

Then, suddenly, he was there.

Barnabas entered a room packed out with gentiles. They were so rowdy and noisy! "Reverence" was not part of their experience. They were completely uninhibited. As they ate (no Jew could ever overlook this), they did so with dirty hands. No Jewish prayer. Nothing. Just eating and rejoicing in the Lord.

Their clothes were not like Jewish clothing. Nor did they seem as clean. Purification was another thing absent from their heritage and their conduct. The length of their hair, by Jewish standards, was an abomination. And, to top it off, there was this one gnawing thought: not a single person in this room had ever been circumcised! That, for any Jew, was hard to take.

Barnabas was suddenly in a different world, and he knew it!!

Maybe, on second thought, these people should not be encouraged to go on in the Lord. If they continued, what on earth might happen? They had no Hebrew heritage to guide them. They had no strong moral fiber. In a word, they were "loose." If Barnabas encouraged them to go on with the Lord in this free way, something terribly different from the Jewish church was going to blossom. What might it eventually look like? There was no guarantee of what might happen if a *gentile* church was allowed to get started. The thought *was* both frightening *and* exciting.

But there it was on every face. As Barnabas looked around the room, there could be no doubt. He could see it in their smiles, hear it in their voices. Christ was their Savior. They *knew* the Lord Jesus. They were redeemed!

It was time for Barnabas to speak. What would he do? The decision he had to make at this moment was unprecedented in all the history of the Jewish faith. Would something *not* Hebrew be allowed to live? Would he encourage these people to go on? Call the whole thing off? Make some corrections here and there? At least take them out and have them circumcised? What, Barnabas, Son of Exhortation, you who have been called "a good man, full of the Holy Spirit," what will you do?

Barnabas stood up. You could almost hear his thoughts: "Well, the Lord started this, I didn't. If He started it, He can finish it." He opened his mouth. . . .

"And he exhorted them all to remain faithful to the Lord and to continue in their faith." And after those gentiles heard this, even more of them believed! And even more, they all rejoiced.

On that day, in that meeting, the church in Antioch was born.

24

Needed: One Co-Worker

For the next few days Barnabas was doubtlessly a restless man. He now faced a difficult choice; no, much more than difficult. Unknown to him, human history would pivot on his decision.

If Barnabas elected to remain in Antioch, he would need help. But perhaps he should just go home to Jerusalem. What business did *he* have raising up a church? After all, no one had actually *sent* him to Antioch to do that. He had come simply to observe and probably to report back to the Apostles. But a lot had happened, more than he could have ever believed. He now found himself in a dilemma.

Barnabas counted his options.

He could send word back to Jerusalem, asking one or two of the Apostles to come up to Antioch to join him; or he could go back home to Jerusalem, give his report, ask some Apostles to go to Antioch, and he would stay home; or . . . he could forget Jerusalem, stay in Antioch himself, and dare raise up the first gentile church!

Barnabas had several things to consider in all these possibilities. For one thing, Greek was *not* the native tongue of any of the Apostles. (Greek *was* Barnabas' native tongue.) On the other hand, Barnabas was not the only one in Jerusalem who could speak Greek. (But *he* had been sent here.) Probably he ought to go back. On the other hand it really *was* a *very* long way back to Jerusalem. (Three hundred miles, a twenty to thirty day journey.)

Barnabas knew, though, that *none* of these things touched the heart of the issue.

The fact was he had a deep and inexplicable burden. That burden had to do with Jerusalem and with the gentiles. To Barnabas, something was not quite right about all the old Jewish influences the believers in Judea were carrying over into their new faith. This carry-over may not have existed in those first days after Pentecost; but, eventually, from living in the midst of all their past religious heritage, the Jerusalem believers had unconsciously slipped back. After all, the Judean believers were surrounded by a temple, rituals, forms, traditions and teachings, plus the unseen pressure of national pride. Judean believers did not seem to ever become fully aware that in Christ they had been set free from all religious systemization.

Barnabas made his decision.

In making it, he did something totally contrary to proper order. He decided *not* to go back to Jerusalem! He seemed not too hurried to send that report back to the Apostles! Without consultation, he took the entire Antioch situation into his own hands. (This may have seemed like outright rebellion, but please remember: the Apostles had sent him there; he had thirteen years of church life under his tunic, and the reason the Apostles had sent him was because they trusted his judgment. As soon as you have Barnabas' qualifications, feel free to do what he did. On top of this, and even more important, Barnabas had the Lord's clear sense to do what he did.)

At this point in his dilemma, Barnabas remembered that man named Saul. He remembered Saul's fifteen-day visit to Jerusalem. He recalled that Saul, though steeped in the ancient traditions, declared a gospel wholly free of Jewish influence. He remembered that day in the Libertine synagogue.

Barnabas needed help. But he would not go to Judea to get it.

Barnabas decided to make a quick eighty mile trip up to Tarsus to see if he could find Saul. (Saul, you recall, had moved back home to Tarsus three years ago to escape a plot in Jerusalem against his life.) The town of Tarsus was fairly close to Antioch. Perhaps Saul was still there. And maybe, just maybe, he would agree to come back to Antioch with Barnabas. So, setting out north and west for Tarsus, Barnabas

170

went hunting for a man like-minded to labor with him in the work that lay ahead.

With that simple decision began one of the greatest turns of history.

25

Tentmakers Two

Barnabas trudged through the gates of Saul's home town. Finding Saul, though, appears to have been somewhat difficult. Saul was still very much in the "wasted years," the "hidden stage" of his life; finding him turned into a hunting expedition.

What Barnabas beheld, as he combed Tarsus for Saul, was one of the key cities of the richly fertile Cilicia plain. The town was located in the southwest corner of a small area called Asia Minor. The Mediterranean Sea lay twelve miles to the south, but the city actually had an inland harbor . . . man made! North of the city some eighteen miles lay the gorges and cliffs of the Taurus mountains. These mountains arched westward in a semi-circle around the city reaching almost to the sea. In winter the peaks were a snow-capped spectacular. Down through the gorges, during the spring and summer thaw, poured the Cydnus River. This river made a narrow, swift journey through the city, ending in the artificial harbor, and there opened the harbor for navigation during the warm months of the year.

The market place Barnabas walked through was dominated by rows of pagan temples. The city of Tarsus was an amalgamation of Hittites, Greeks, Assyrians, Persians, Macedonians and indigenous Cilicians. From what he saw, Barnabas knew that Saul knew gentiles! Saul, like himself, had grown up in a city utterly removed from the dominant culture and society of Judaism. Having been raised in this town, Saul had to be bilingual . . . speaking Hebrew at home and Greek in the markets.

It was here in the market place Barnabas undoubtedly watched the master tentmakers ply their trade. Barnabas, a tentmaker himself, could watch the craftsmen weave a cloth made from the hair of the large, black, long-haired goats that grazed on the slopes of the Taurus mountains. This tent material was called "cilicium" and was used by caravans, nomads and soldiers throughout all Asia Minor.

Perhaps it was here, among the tentmakers of Tarsus, that Barnabas was finally able to get information about Saul.

Of this we are certain, he eventually located Saul.

The two men sat and talked. Saul listened attentively as Barnabas recounted the spectacular, mind-boggling news of what had happened at Caesarea and Antioch. After the story had been recounted, Barnabas dropped the bomb, "Saul, would you be willing to return to Antioch with me?" It appears Saul had no hesitations about agreeing. He knew he had been called to proclaim the Gospel to the gentiles. The Lord had called him to this on the very day he had been converted.

So marks the beginning of a relationship between two men which will last for seven long years: a relationship which will be filled with suffering and with glory, but one of the most remarkable in all history.

What exactly had Saul been doing these last three years in Tarsus? You recall that he had spent the first three years after his conversion out in the desert, alone, getting to know the Lord–doing nothing. Well, it seems he had been doing the same thing during these second three years in Tarsus. Saul had spent six years getting to know his Lord.*

Saul closed out all his affairs in Tarsus and made ready to leave for Antioch. Never again would Tarsus be "home" for Saul. The two men set out together for the five day trip back to Antioch.

Saul got to the church in Antioch just in time "to be there from the beginning." The church in Antioch was noted for proclaiming the gospel, and it seems Saul was put to work doing just that from the very outset.

There is a good chance we even know where Saul lived during his four year stay in Antioch. It is very likely he lived

*There is virtually nothing but conjecture that says he ministered in Tarsus. Barnabas had to "hunt" to even find Saul in Tarsus. He had *not* entered public ministry.

with Mr. and Mrs. Simeon Niger and their two sons Rufus and Alexander. Mrs. Niger seems to have taken it upon herself to look after the needs of this thirty-three year old bachelor.

God had sovereignly prepared these two men. Their preparation was of almost unparalleled significance in church history. Then what manner of men were these two? What had they been through? How had God prepared them for the work He now laid before them? Look closely at the answer. You can see the principles by which God operates when preparing men for *His work.* (*His* work, by the way, is the church.) See what God puts in a man He wants to make a minister of the Gospel. Barnabas is a "worker" in Antioch right now. He will someday become an Apostle. So his life *really* bears observing. *Behold* how strict that preparation is.

Look at Barnabas.

Barnabas is (by the age we gave him) now forty-three years old. Joseph-Barnabas comes from Cyprus. He was born and raised an islander. (Cyprus is about 150 miles out in the Mediterranean Sea, due west of Antioch.) He is a Jew, but like Saul, his native tongue is Greek. Barnabas is from the ancient Hebrew tribe of Levi, the tribe from which the Jewish priests are chosen, but Barnabas has never been a priest. Nonetheless, the religious schooling of his youth, by virtue of the fact that he was Levite, was much more exacting than the religious training of most Jewish boys—just in case he had ever chosen to be a priest. Barnabas knows his Jewish religion well. He knows its traditions and theology. He has studied Moses and the prophets. (In other words, he knows his scrolls!) Beyond this, Barnabas has been raised in a wealthy family. After becoming a believer, though, he made himself poor. He has learned abandonment.

In the year 30 a.d., Barnabas decided to leave the isle of Cyprus to visit Jerusalem and participate in the annual feast of Pentecost. He was just one of thousands of visitors to arrive in the city that year. Like so many others, he witnessed the events of that day and doubtlessly heard Peter speak. He was fully converted to Christ and gave himself utterly to the Lord.

That was God's preparation in Barnabas' life *until* conversion. What did God place in Barnabas' life *after* conversion? What does God put in the life of a man to prepare that man to raise up the church?

First of all, notice that Barnabas experienced the daily life of the church. For eight years he was a simple brother in the church in Jerusalem . . . and that was all. Every day he met with the other believers when they gathered in homes. He sang, prayed, praised and fellowshipped. His experience was an exact parallel to that of Stephen and Phillip!*

Barnabas, like Stephen and Phillip, belonged to that *second group* raised up after the Apostles. He was one of those new breed, servants of the Lord who had never met the Lord personally . . . yet knew Him well.

Secondly, Barnabas had been in the Jerusalem church "from the beginning." This is significant. Though Barnabas did absolutely nothing during that "beginning," he nonetheless got a ring-side seat on what the Apostles did at the beginning. He got the privilege of seeing exactly how the Apostles went about doing things, from the very first day! He saw, experientially, how men deal with "beginnings" in the Lord's work. Barnabas had the privilege of watching the Apostles lay the foundation of the first church ever to exist on the face of the earth. Thirteen years later this experience was priceless to him. (How to go into Antioch and begin the church from scratch was not a complete mystery to Barnabas.) As you know, the twelve had also learned how to begin a work! They had been with the Lord "from the beginning." Barnabas was the third motion in this drama . . . with Saul, a fourth motion, standing there watching every move Barnabas made in launching the Antioch church!

Thirdly, Barnabas sat at the feet of the Apostles as they taught daily at Solomon's Porch. This is something different from experiencing the church. Men may experience the life of the church and never sit at the feet of Apostles. What the Apostles did in teaching at the temple was distinct from the

---

*Barnabas actually accumulated thirteen years of experience in the church *before* going to Antioch. (Stephen and Phillip had eight before they began to serve the Lord.) At the outset of the Jerusalem persecution he went into Judea. After the persecution he returned to Jerusalem. From there he went to Antioch. That covers a period of thirteen years.

experience of living in the church. Barnabas heard *everything* the Apostles said for eight years! Of course, they had an incredible amount to say! He learned what they had learned while being with Jesus! But more. Barnabas did not just sit and listen. He *experienced* the things they taught!

He experienced. He watched. He listened. He learned. Look closely and you will see that Barnabas' relationship to the Apostles for eight years was very much like *their* relationship to the Lord for four years! From the beginning they had watched and they had listened, but they had *done* very little.

So it was with Barnabas. For a decade Barnabas worked no miracles, gave no messages, did not chase off to the ends of the earth. He had not even gotten outside the city limits of Jerusalem.

Next, Barnabas was given utterly to the church and to the Lord. You can be sure of this! At one point Barnabas sold all his real estate holdings, and everything else he had of value, and gave the money to the Apostles. Now if that is nothing else, *that* is exciting! *That* is bold! *That* will change your life . . . leaving you with no chance to backtrack!

But the most important fact is this: Barnabas daily experienced Christ deep in his spirit; every day he met in homes and fellowshipped with the other saints; he got to know Christ! He also got to know the church.

You see what God put in Barnabas' life. It is a man full of this experience whom God put His hand on to raise up the first gentile church! *This* man, with *this* experience, raised up one of the *four* great churches of the first century. *This* is the experience God still desires to put men through. This kind of experience, and this alone, is the proper foundation upon which ministry is to be built. There is no such thing as a "crash program" when it is truly *God* who is preparing a man.

One last thing. If Barnabas was thirty when converted, he was forty-three when he began to minister. He was not exactly a young man. But mark this: the late thirties, the early forties, was a fairly typical age during the first century for a man to *begin* ministering!!

So this is Barnabas. This is the man whom the Lord selected and prepared to come to Antioch. God selected twelve Apostles to raise up the first church on earth. It has fallen Barnabas' lot to single-handedly raise up the first *gentile* church. For the next four years he will work diligently to build that church in Antioch. And he will do one whale of a job of it, too!

Saul, in the meantime, will *start* getting the type of experience Barnabas acquired years ago! First, he will have the privilege of being in Antioch "from the beginning," just as Barnabas was in Jerusalem "from the beginning." Saul will sit at the feet of Barnabas; and for the next four years he will get his first real dose of the powerful daily experience of church life.

Saul will watch; he will help; he will learn; but Barnabas will lead.

The work Saul did for Christ in Antioch was *all* done under the direction of Barnabas. For the next four years he would learn much from that brother. He would be a student. Saul began learning from Barnabas what Barnabas had learned in thirteen years of church life; he learned the things Barnabas had learned in having sat at the feet of the Apostles for eight years.

This was God's way to prepare men in the first century . . . so it must be again.

The Lord is moving onward and upward.

It is about 43 a.d.

Some visitors from Jerusalem are about to drop in.

26

Famine, Death, and Triumph

His name is Agabus. He is a prophet* and the first person ever to pay a visit to the church in Antioch from the church in Jerusalem. He has come for a very special purpose: he has a message to deliver which he has already delivered to the believers in Judea. It is a word from the Lord, and it is important enough to cause him to travel 300 miles so that Antioch will also hear the message.

Who is Agabus? You have met him before, right after the day of Pentecost. At that time, at age twenty-five, he didn't look very promising. Today he is a much respected brother. Of course now he is almost forty. (It does take a little time!)

The Holy Spirit has made Agabus a prophet. And what is a prophet? First, of all, forget the twentieth century concept. A prophet is *not* a man who goes around predicting future events all the time. There simply are not *that many*

*A *prophet!* New things have been happening in Jerusalem again. The last time we looked, the church in Jerusalem could claim twelve Apostles and one evangelist. Now here is something called a "prophet." As the Jerusalem church has matured, yet one more gift has been manifested among the men who were first saved on the day of Pentecost. And please note, it has taken only fourteen years!

The fact that God was taking a long time to produce what He wanted is very important. It is important to you, a twentieth century believer. Long ago church life vanished from the face of the earth. Today God yearns to recover that life—which means that He must do a work of restoration. Will the Lord take less time to restore than He did at the genesis of the church? God took a lot of time in the beginning, and you can be sure that He will take *at least* that much time again. Do you realize that could mean waiting fourteen years just to get a prophet—mind you, just *one* prophet—who would be the product of a true experience of church life!

future events worth predicting. A prophet is one who reveals Christ. A prophet is one who speaks for God in the place of God. Yes, it is true that this particular prophet does predict future events . . . occasionally. But predictions are rare for any prophet, in any age. Mostly, a prophet speaks for God; and mostly, when God speaks, God declares Christ.

Agabus happened to be doing the rare thing when he was in Antioch. The Lord had shown him some very disconcerting events which were to come. He had told Agabus that a famine was about to spread across the whole earth and that the churches should get ready for it. The effects were to be especially disastrous in Jerusalem. (In fact, it appears the famine had already hit Jerusalem. Agabus seems to have come to Antioch simply to tell the church that the famine was on its way.)

Why was Jerusalem in particular to be hit so hard by the famine? For one thing, the church there was never wealthy, even in normal years. Jerusalem was an unusual city. It was more of an international tourist attraction than a normal metropolis. Its population was unstable; steady employment was always a problem; jobs were seasonal; wages were low; housing was scarce and expensive, becoming even worse during religious celebrations.

You might say Jerusalem was antiquity's version of a convention center or a city hosting a World's Fair. Every year, three times a year, when visitors poured in from all over the Roman Empire, Jerusalem was packed to the walls. Its population increased six fold almost overnight. Many of these visitors, of course, were Jewish Christians. Naturally, the church in Jerusalem hosted these brothers and sisters while they were in town. Any financial surplus the Jerusalem church ever had was probably wiped out during these festivals.

Another local economic factor was the farmland surrounding the city. It was not especially fertile, as was the land around Antioch. In a good year, Jerusalem's local crops were adequate for the needs of its own population with only a small exportable surplus. Jerusalem would never be able to withstand a long drought. Antioch, on the other hand, would be able to live from the large grain surplus stored from the good years.

This meant that as of right now, Jerusalem was out of grain, whereas there was still grain in the fields all around Antioch; enough for the Antioch believers to go out and buy for their own future needs, and enough to meet Jerusalem's present and future needs, too.

If Agabus' prediction was correct, then everyone in Judea was in for a long period of suffering. The Antioch church would not only be able to get ready for the drought but would also be able to help Jerusalem. If the prediction was true, there was no question that the Antioch church would gladly do this very thing.

If the prediction was true! But was it? Or was Agabus just talking some wild nonsense? Could Agabus be trusted?

In our century, predictions of future events are about ten cents a bushel. There is a new one almost every week. Few, hardly any, in fact, turn out to be correct. So the question is, how could men such as Barnabas listen to, much less believe, what Agabus was predicting? The answer is important. Unlike any of our modern-day oracles, Agabus had already been tested and proven by God and by the church to be a trustworthy servant.

How proven? By living through fourteen years of the fires of church life. That, dear reader, is a lot of testing! Agabus was known to be a faithful man: he accurately presented Christ whenever he stood to speak; he unveiled Christ to the church; he spoke for God. Eventually, as the years rolled on, he even made a few out-and-out predictions . . . which *always* came true!

After a while, the church realized that it could rely on Agabus' accuracy. But don't get the idea that this made Agabus something super in the church. He was just another brother, one who had lived in very close quarters with other saints for many years. His personality, shortcomings and failures, his strengths and his character were all well known. No, the church did not grovel at the sight of "Agabus the Prophet" when he walked into the room. He was not a "super believer." (That kind of attitude toward the Lord's servants didn't come into being for centuries.) Church life keeps hero worship snuffed out. The church is not made up of spiritual giants, just survivors! Agabus was just another member of the body in Jerusalem. As it had been with Stephen, as with all men in the church, the Lord's people had confidence in Agabus *despite* the fact that he had been completely exposed throughout the years. That is the glory of church life!

Furthermore, Barnabas knew all about Agabus. After all, he had lived with him in Jerusalem for at least eight years when they were both young converts. They had been through the fires together. Barnabus *knew* Agabus!

It is no surprise, then, that Barnabas and the church in Antioch accepted Agabus' word at face value. Jerusalem was going to need help, and even though the gentile believers had never met their Jewish brothers, they just naturally loved them and wanted to help. So they rolled up their sleeves and set about to prepare for a world-wide famine that would last for years. A pretty big task for a church less than two years old.

Please keep in mind, this is not just some story. This really happened. A whole church got together and made ready for a famine. This was not a lot of individuals getting ready for a catastrophe. This was the church corporate, moving as one. First century believers had only one activity in life: the church! An individual life lived 90% alone and 10% "at church" was unknown in that day. All of living, all 18 waking hours a day, was church life.

The Antioch church was going through this famine *together!* For them, problems, joys, famine, family, church, and even *life,* were all one and the same.

Can you imagine something like this taking place today? Imagine a pastor walking into the pulpit on Easter Sunday morning with the church secretary, the minister of education, the song leader and the janitor all standing beside him, and announcing that it is time for the congregation to pool their resources and incomes and get ready for an upcoming depression. Can you imagine the reaction! His words would have all the chance of an igloo on the equator!

Or imagine that a genuine twentieth century prophet (?) predicted an immanent economic disaster before a group of Christians today. Imagine that everyone in the room *knew* his prediction would prove to be correct. You can be sure it would be every man for himself . . . with everyone rushing home to store his own supply of food, and with the business-minded believer calling up his stock broker to figure out how he could make a killing on the stock market because of his inside tip from God. That is *exactly* what men today would do in a situation similar to the one in Antioch. May the Lord preserve us!

How did Antioch prepare for a famine, anyway? And how did they send help to Jerusalem? We do not know their exact methods. But it is certain that no one was thinking more of his individual survival than he was of corporate survival. Everybody may have simply pooled their resources, saved up a large amount of money and sent it to Jerusalem while continuing to store up grain for themselves. But that is unlikely. What good was money in Jerusalem if there was no grain to buy? Probably the Antioch church did the most practical and the most economical thing: they bought and stored their grain during the year of abundance so they could distribute it during the famine.

Here's how it was almost certainly handled.

The Antioch believers were poor, but they pooled all they had plus all they made, until there was enough money saved to send some brothers up the Orontes River to buy grain. This was done repeatedly, storing the grain each time until there was a considerable supply. Then arrangements were made to ship it to Judea via Joppa and from there to haul it by mule to Jerusalem.

Antioch acted very swiftly, especially for such a young church. Once the grain was ready for shipment, the church selected two men to escort it to Jerusalem. One of them, of course, was Barnabas. The second man chosen was Saul.

So, Barnabas is going to Jerusalem! Now that could be interesting. No! Barnabas in Jerusalem? That could be *dangerous!*

Barnabas is finally going to make his report about Antioch to the Apostles! The trip *could* turn out to be a disaster. Just consider the situation. Barnabas had not seen the Apostles in well over a year. In the meantime he had taken it upon himself to raise up the church in Antioch. That probably would not get him in too much trouble. But there was something he *had* done which could possibly get him boiled in olive oil.

What was that? He had taken a stand *against* circumcision, that was what!

One day someone in Antioch must have come up to Barnabas and asked, "Shall we tell all these new converts to get circumcised?" What a question! To Barnabas must go the credit for one of the most revolutionary decisions in all religious history, when he faced that question squarely and replied, "No!" That decision was precedent shattering. The gentiles did not first need to be circumcised to become Christians. This was an act of pure heresy in the eyes of some—a virtual break with the faith itself.

Now Barnabas was going back to Jerusalem. He would have to face the consequences of his decision. He knew, as surely as Jews have rules, that he was going to be asked to give an account of himself, to justify his unprecedented decision. Anything could happen. He had no idea how it would go. He could be praised, roasted or replaced for what he had done.

If Barnabas is in trouble and if the Apostles challenge his actions, will he stand up to them? The answer to that is an unqualified "No!" Barnabas will have to give in completely. He owes those twelve men all he is, all he knows, all he believes. A humble brother like Barnabas just doesn't stand against the twelve. (Neither does anyone else.) There is no question that if the Apostles had told Barnabas to go back to Antioch and begin circumcising the converts, he would have given in. But Barnabas also knew he would stand his ground as long as he could if he was questioned. He would do his best to turn the tide against legalism.

This trip, therefore, gave every promise of being a first class showdown.

What Barnabas did not know was that God had decided to postpone the showdown and had already arranged the circumstances in Jerusalem so that his arrival there would go almost unnoticed.

And what was happening right now in Jerusalem? To fully understand the answer to *that* question we will have to take a look at some of Judea's past history.

Back in 4 b.c., Judea had been ruled by its own King, one Herod the Great. After Herod died the Roman Emperor

Augustus decided not to let Judea continue having its own king. He decided instead to rule that land by means of Roman Procurators, a series of which then ruled Judea until 41 a.d.

In 41 a.d., the Emperor Caligula decided to again test the merits of a king for the Jews, so he appointed Herod Agrippa I (grandson of Herod the Great) ro rule over all Palestine. Of course the religious Jews were very pleased with this decision. For one thing a king might be the very thing they needed to stop the increasing return of disciples to Jerusalem. Yes, the disciples had recently (44 a.d.) been multiplying in the Holy City. They were meeting again in homes. The Jews had been watching and were getting uneasy once again.

The last time the Jews had moved to snuff out "the way," they were under the rule of a Roman Procurator. Whenever they had wanted to stone a man to death, they first had to try him in court, find him guilty, and then get Roman permission to kill him—permission they very rarely received. But now, in the spring of 44 a.d., they had their own king; and with a king, they could revert to ancient Jewish custom. The Talmud allowed the king of Judea the power to execute a man by the sword—no trial, no red tape, not even stones. It could be done any time, with no more prerequisite than a word from the king himself. At last they had a quick way to stop the church. Only one question was left: would their king, who lived in Caesarea, cooperate?

The Jews went to Herod Agrippa I to find out. They pleaded with him to strike at the very heart of this new heresy. Herod listened attentively. Here was an opportunity to win favor with the leading Jews of his new realm. Their request was obviously very dear to them. He agreed to help them and went right to work.

In one swift, unexpected and shocking move, Herod ordered the arrest of the Apostle James, and *then* ordered him to be *executed* immediately, without trial! It was done. The religious Jews were ecstatic. At last one of the Apostles had been caught and killed! For the church, it was the saddest, blackest day since Stephen's death. Herod, in turn, had no idea it was going to be so easy to win so much favor from the Sanhedrin. If killing James pleased them, what would killing Peter do! Herod was already planning to visit Jerusalem during the celebration of the Passover, so why not make a big affair of it?

Herod ordered Peter's arrest. He then scheduled the Apostle to be executed during Passover—sort of a grand finale to the weekend. Fourteen years to the day after the death of the Lord Jesus, Peter was scheduled to be killed.

The church had gone through the persecution of 38-40 a.d., without losing a single Apostle. Now in the persecution of 44 a.d., they were about to lose *two*. It looked like the church was to be plunged into another blood bath.

The church entered into intense prayer. In homes all over the city saints began to pray for Peter's release. God heard their prayers and sent an angel to unlock the prison doors. Peter escaped in a walk, but not an hour too soon. He made his exit the very morning of his scheduled execution.

Herod was furious. He ordered the guards who had been in charge of Peter to be killed. He was still in a fury when he left Jerusalem to get back to Caesarea for some Roman games and festivities which he had scheduled there.

God was also angry. He was angry with Herod, who would have found it difficult to believe that he would be dead inside a week.

It happened this way.

On the day set for the opening of the Roman games in Caesarea, a delegation of men arrived from the cities of Tyre and Sidon for the purpose of trying to see Herod. Their mission was urgent. Tyre and Sidon had sent this delegation to Herod because they were running short of food. They needed grain and they needed it badly. But Herod was prejudiced against their region of the country, and they knew it. They were desperate to get an appointment to see him and to make peace. They bribed one of the king's aides, a fellow named Blastus, to get the necessary audience.

Herod agreed to see them. He scheduled a speech for them, to be delivered out of doors and early in the morning on the second day of the Roman games. Sure enough King Herod dressed himself in a royal robe made of silver twine, stepped out into the morning light, sat down on his throne, and began to speak. As the sun rose, its rays fell directly on his robe. His oration was breathtaking. So was his appearance. In the morning light his robe seemed to be ablaze! The audience began to cry, "A god has spoken."

Herod did not refute a word of this praise! To any Jew, this was an overt act of blasphemy. Nonetheless, he just sat there as if to say, "So, you have finally figured it out!"

As God watched this new competition, He decided that a test was in order. He sent an angel to visit the new "god." Immediately Herod found himself stricken with a horrible intestinal disease. It seems that he could not muster up quite enough divinity to cure himself, and after an agonizing five days was taken out and buried.* He died (very undivinely) of worms!

The Jews had lost their second major ally in their efforts to destroy the church.

It was sometime during all these hair-raising events that Barnabas and Saul arrived in Jerusalem. Of course, no one could pay a whole lot of attention to them in the midst of such tense, uncertain times. Certainly the church was thankful for the grain, and surely they were glad to see Barnabas and Saul. The Jerusalem church even seems to have openly acknowledged that Antioch had a real, genuine church in it.**

Everyone rejoiced at the things going on in Antioch, but things were just too chaotic for anyone to think to ask Barnabas the *big question* . . . about circumcision. God, by unusual ways, had seen to it that the inevitable showdown was postponed. But it would come!

This must have been a very frustrating trip for Saul. This was his second trip to Jerusalem since becoming a Christian,

---

*When the Emperor Caligula heard of Agrippa's death, he looked around for another qualified king, and finding none but Herod's seventeen year old son, decided to go back to using Roman Procurators to rule Palestine.

**Mark that, Jerusalem recognized Antioch not as a local sect, but as a genuine church despite the fact it was not in the orthodox Judean flow of things. You will recall that wherever a church had been born in Judea, an Apostle had always gone to add his approval. But no Apostle had ever visited Antioch. Despite this fact, the church in Antioch, raised up completely outside the flow of God's work in Judea, was recognized as a sister church.

and he still hadn't met any of the Apostles except Peter, or even gone to a meeting of the church. The church wasn't meeting and the Apostles were still in hiding. All the two men could do, under the circumstances, was deliver their gift to the elders and go back home.

Before we leave Jerusalem, there are a few things we need to note. God is still working in the Jerusalem church. This is still the place God is using to give birth to things totally new. On the day the church was born, it started with Apostles. Later the church got an evangelist, then prophets and now, last of all, they have something called elders.

The Holy Spirit has raised up Apostles, 30 a.d.; evangelists, 38 a.d.; prophets, 43 a.d.; and now about 44 a.d., *yet another* function in the church: elders!*

What is an elder, anyway?

And why so long in coming? Fourteen years, no less!

First of all, elders are men appointed by the Holy Spirit. Repeat, only the Holy Spirit chooses elders. They are chosen by Him to oversee the *administrative* matters of the church. Elders are not Apostles: they do not raise up churches. They are not prophets: they do not speak for God nor reveal Christ. Yes, an elder can be both a prophet and an elder, but being an elder does not automatically make him one who ministers. If an elder does speak the Word of God to the church, he does it *not* as an elder but as a simple brother in the church or as a prophet.

Next, elders do not lead the meetings. They don't come out of some little anteroom right before a meeting begins, march down the aisles, sit down on the front row (each carrying a scroll under his arm), whisper secretly to one another and then, to begin the meeting, announce the opening hymn.

That is not an elder. *That* is an abomination!

*Once the Lord gave elders to the church in Jerusalem, He would soon begin to raise up elders in other churches. Churches coming *after* Jerusalem didn't take as long to get elders as Jerusalem did. But please always remember that no matter how quickly God gave elders to later churches, it took fifteen years to get that first genuine set. In a situation of *restoration*, that first set of the genuine article will *also* come very slowly!

No! Elders have nothing to do with *meetings* of the church.

Elders are not Apostles; they therefore do not raise up churches, and they do not have as much authority as an Apostle. Neither are they prophets: *as elders,* they do not minister in the church. (As brothers they may, but *not as* elders.) They have virtually no part in leading church meetings. Then what are they?

They *are* the administrative authority of the church *if* an Apostle is not present.

Raising up churches belongs to Apostles.

Administration belongs to Apostles. . . or to elders if Apostles are not present.

Ministry belongs to prophets, teachers, Apostles and to the body itself. (Yes the *body*—the church—ministers to *itself* just as Apostles, prophets and teachers minister to the church.) Eldering is confined almost exclusively to matters *outside* the meetings. You will recall the church in Jerusalem had two places of meeting: Solomon's Porch, where the *Apostles* were in charge of the meetings, and the homes, where *nobody* was in charge.

Furthermore, did you know that not all churches had elders? That seems inconsistent! God is like that. He will appear to establish an unveering principle, one you can put into a neat, tight little outline, then He comes along and smashes it with one of those glorious exceptions of His. He is an elusive God. You *cannot* put your Lord or His ways into a system.

To illustrate: there is no record that the church in Antioch *ever* had elders. For instance, when the grain was sent from Antioch to Jerusalem, it was very specifically sent from the *church* in Antioch to the *elders* in Jerusalem! Jerusalem had elders. Antioch did not.

One last question.

Why did it take the Lord well over a decade to give the church its very first elders? The answer: *beginning* always takes longer.

This is a fact which sorely needs to be seen. Unfortunately in our age Christians who have moved out of church buildings and meet in homes will almost invariably start selecting "elders" after meeting together for only a few months. People just don't *select* elders. Eldership isn't recovered in three months. That is not recovery at all. A true elder, a man produced from the fires of church life after years and years of waiting and testing, just doesn't exist on earth today. God will take just as long to *recover* eldership today as He did to begin it in the first century.

The Lord knew that the first group of men to be called *elders* would be a prototype for all churches to come. So He took His time. Those men had to be perfect examples. Therefore the Holy Spirit took long years to put experience, life, maturity, wisdom, patience and love into them. Then the Holy Spirit allowed their function as elders to emerge.

There is a second reason it took some time for elders to come into being. An elder must be local. A man cannot be an elder of a church if he is new in town, even if he is a gifted, spiritual brother. To be an elder a man must be a long-standing resident of the church and the town he is in. Elders cannot be imported ready-made. Great tragedy comes to the Lord's people when this is ignored. You recall that when the Jerusalem church was born, almost no one in it was a local resident of Jerusalem. All those non-local Jews had to become local by living there a long time before they could be qualified for such things as eldership.

There is perhaps a third reason elders were so long in appearing. It has to do with Apostles. The church in Jerusalem had twelve Apostles. That is a world's record. Twelve Apostles in one church. No other church ever had that many Apostles in it. There were no elders, prophets or evangelists. There was the church, plus the Apostles, plus nothing. Those twelve men more or less dominated the whole scene. They were in charge of both ministry and administration. That role was correct; and it was important. Why?

First of all, during those first eight years men got to observe the way the Apostles carried out church administration. They saw brokenness, tenderness, patience with authority. The twelve Apostles were the world's first example of what eldership was supposed to be. May the Lord save us from men who have never seen true eldership humbly lived out *before their very eyes* previous to the time they themselves become elders. If men miss this precious lesson, you can be sure that when they become "elders," they will eventually turn out to be tyrants, not elders. You have to *see* brokenness and tenderness and patience. You have to see it exercised on *you,* and then you will have some small foundation in your own life which the Holy Spirit can use as he begins to give you some responsibilities.

Second, after eight years, the Apostles finally began to spend time outside Jerusalem. They went out visiting all those new churches in Judea. That meant that little by little, administration of local matters had to be taken care of by others. The Apostles simply were not around as much as they once had been. So, in 42 or 43 a.d., as the Jerusalem church came back to life, administration began to shift out of the hands of the Apostles into the hands of other men. It was from these circumstances that the Holy Spirit brought forth the function of elders.

So it was that around 43 to 44 a.d. men became aware of something new on earth: eldership.

Once God had given elders to the church, it became clear to everyone that He intended virtually all churches to eventually have such men. It was also clear that the Holy Spirit alone would select those men and raise them up.

Perchance you are a Christian who meets in a "home group." Where does that leave you? What chance have you of seeing a true recovery of eldership? None! Unless your group was raised up by men of Apostolic stature in the first place. Without that prerequisite, the question is academic. Secondly, you should expect to dig in and wait one or two decades for those first elders. Thirdly, while you are waiting, you can expect to pass through some really hair-raising experiences that will shake and sift and expose everyone. If you survive several such experiences, no one will have to ask who the elders are. They will be evident to everyone. Unfortunately 4,999,999 home groups out of 5,000,000 don't have the necessary beginning (though almost all think they do), and virtually none survive the first three years . . . much less a decade.

Enough about eldership for now. Let's return to Barnabas and Saul.

Their work complete, Barnabas and Saul prepared to return to Antioch.

Just before returning home, it seems Barnabas stopped to visit his sister Mary. (Her home was one of the gathering places for the Jerusalem church.) While there, Mary's son, John Mark, expressed a very keen desire to go with his uncle to Antioch; he even wanted to live there. Barnabas approved the idea.

We will hear more of John Mark. (If he was ten years old when Pentecost took place, he would be about twenty-five years old now.) So, Barnabas and Saul have a young man with them as they begin their journey home.

The trio arrived back in Antioch in the year 45 a.d. and gave a report to the church on their trip to Jerusalem.

The year 46 a.d. will pass uneventfully. In 47 a.d., though, a simple prayer meeting in Antioch will alter the course of western civilization.

It is time now to turn our attention more fully to Antioch because, from this point on, the main work of God on earth will be with the gentiles.

27

Gentile Church Life

Church life in Antioch! What was it like?

It was free, loose, gentile to the core and very evangelistic!

But most of all, it was different. Even its beginning was different.

The church in Antioch belongs in the line of churches that came out of Jerusalem. You might say it was the *last* church to come from the *Jerusalem line.*

You recall that out of Jerusalem, which was a *genesis* church, came over 100 churches. All these churches were established by *transplanting* whole groups of Christians bodily to a new city. The church in Antioch was founded this way. But for Antioch that's where the Jerusalem pattern ended.

There were several reasons Antioch was the turning point between two lines of God's work. First of all, the dispersed Christians who first went to Antioch found themselves in gentile territory. Antioch was in no way a Jewish town.

(God will soon be raising up a second *line* of churches, as you will see. We will refer to this newer work as the *Antioch line:* these churches will all come out of the church in Antioch.)

Secondly, unlike in Judea, the group which came to Antioch was extremely small. Too small. And the gentiles' response to their Gospel was large. Too large! The poor Jews were deluged. That little group of probably no more than ten or twelve at maximum was simply engulfed by new gentile believers. If the number had been about equally divided, half

Jews, half gentiles, the expression of the church in Antioch might have turned out to be just another Jewish expression of the church islanded in a gentile city. That would have been a tragedy. Fortunately God kept such a thing from happening. From the outset there were just too many gentiles. The Judean *"form"* never had a chance. Rowdy, noisy, irreverent gentile meetings took the day. The Jerusalem-Judean way of meeting was never even seen in Antioch.

The fact is, that little band of Jews who proclaimed Christ in Antioch showed remarkable wisdom. To them must go the main credit for the first *different* church on this earth. During those first, all important days, they had the sense to stand back and let the gentiles find their own natural ways of expressing Christ. Let's go back and meet some of those audacious men who founded the church in Antioch. We know only three of them by name, but that is enough to give us some insight into what God was doing in Antioch.

First, meet Simeon Niger, or Simeon the Black.

Simeon is a Negro, coming originally from Cyrene, Africa. He is almost unquestionably the man who carried the Lord's cross on the day of the crucifixion. He was probably a gentile who had become a Jewish proselyte. He was undoubtedly converted to Christ on the day of Pentecost. Eight years later he fled Jerusalem, and by 43 a.d., he had ended up in Antioch. He is married. He has two sons: one is named Alexander—probably because he was born in Alexandria, Egypt; the other is named Rufus, or Redman.

Next meet Manaen.

Manaen has a semitic heritage. Of royal blood, he is related to Herod and was educated in Rome. Manaen, too, was probably in Jerusalem in 30 a.d. and converted at Pentecost. As a result of the persecution he eventually found himself in the little band that moved to Antioch.

Next meet Lucius.

Of Lucius all we know is that he comes from Cyrene, northeast Africa.

When these men first entered Antioch, they had already been Christians for thirteen years. They were just ordinary, simple, run-of-the-mill brothers. They were *not* Apostles, elders, prophets or teachers. Like thousands of their fellows, they were just believers on fire, set loose with the Gospel.

When these three men, plus a handful more, started speaking the Gospel in Antioch they received the warmest response that had *ever* been given to the Gospel. Of course, those gentiles who packed in to hear the Gospel had never been in a religious gathering in all their lives. There was no way on earth for them to know they were supposed to meet the way people in Judea met. They just came together as the type of people they were: gentiles being gentiles. They could have had no other thought. They listened. Some got saved. Then they acted like *saved* gentiles in a gentile meeting! Antiochenes already had the reputation of being a rambunctious, witty people with a good sense of the ridiculous and a love for the satirical. So was born the gentile way of meeting, thought up, created, and produced *by* gentiles: raw-boned, loud, gusty, irreverent, loose, informal and joyous.

But the most wonderful thing about it all was that Lucius, Manaen and Simeon, et al., had the good sense to stand back and let those gentile Christians find their own natural expression!

By the time Barnabas arrived, the damage had been done, the dye cast. Those gentiles still didn't have the vaguest idea how Judeans did things. Something new had been born. Barnabas made sure it stayed that way.

The point is, the church in Antioch was *not* like the church in Jerusalem or the other transplanted churches in Judea. In fact, as the years rolled on, it became clear that God had stepped up a notch when He arrived in Antioch. He had changed course and had begun a higher work than He had ever done before.

There are other unique features about church life in Antioch.

For instance, its lifestyle.

It was probably the first church *not* to practice living in common! (But neither did they go on living the way they had *before* the church came to town!)

Let's look closer.

The church in Antioch, it appears, did not live in common, but rather it lived in clusters—clusters scattered here and there all over the city.

Clusters?

In Antioch there was no reason for the church to live in common; after all everyone who was saved already lived in Antioch. Only about ten didn't! Antioch saints *did* drop "the Greek way of life," however. Everyone seems to have wanted to move close to one another. It also appears that they often ate their meals together. (They may have even lived in common, or at least eaten in common, during the time of the famine.)

This desire to leave your home just to move next door to other saints will not strike you as strange if you ever experience true church life. Christians just naturally want to be surrounded by other believers. You *need* each other. But there was also a practical reason for living in clusters. Antioch was a big city, far too spread out for everyone to walk to some central gathering place every time the church met. Remember, there were no buses or cars. Therefore, all the believers moved around in such a way as to be very near a place to gather. Fair weather or foul, all you had to do was go next door to be with a roomful of fellow believers.

As a result, places like Singon Street (in an area called the Epiphania district, near the Pantheon and Charon's faceless head) gradually became thick with Christians.

The church did gather "all in one place" from time to time, but we have no idea how often. The *small* home meetings and the *large* meetings which were "all in one place" were very different from one another, but they had one thing in common: they were both glorious to be in.

Next was its oneness.

Perhaps the most unique feature of the church in Antioch was its almost incomprehensible *unity*. There is no record that discord was ever known *within* the church in Antioch. Love for one another (and for the Judean saints they had never met) flowed true and deep.

Furthermore, there is no record of any serious persecution of the church from *without* during those early days. Antioch's civil authorities never harassed the believers. On the contrary, from the beginning the populace seems to have given an open door to the Gospel. Amazing when you realize those believers were proclaiming the Gospel of the Kingdom!

That brings us to the next characteristic of this church: it was probably the most evangelistic church of the first century. Proclaiming the Gospel in Antioch was as easy as eating mutton, and the Jewish disciples (Barnabas, Saul, Lucius, Manaen, Simeon and others) made the most of it.

The church was born in a burst of evangelism, a characteristic it never got around to dropping. From the first day, evangelism was the hallmark of the church in Antioch. The Gospel seems to have been proclaimed somewhere in that city every day.

Their constant exercise of evangelism is probably what made it so easy for the Greeks to find and keep their own unique way of meeting. There were always too many new gentiles coming into the meetings for any traditions or rituals to be established.

There were other oddities in the Antioch church.

There were no miracles or fantastic signs in Antioch, as there were in Jerusalem. Antioch mainly grew in just the one way: through the unrelenting proclamation of the Gospel!

Also, the church in Antioch had no elders.

This was indeed unique. It is just about the only church that seems *never* to have gotten around to having administrative overseers.

Why? There are a few very likely reasons. Before you can have elders you just about have to have a series of crises in the church—so that the elders are clearly evidenced. (It takes the *cross* to reveal true eldership in the church. It takes *pressure* to unveil a true love for the church. It takes a *crisis* to reveal who doesn't *panic* under fire.) Antioch never had any significant schism *within* or persecution from *without.*

Another explanation of this unity can perhaps be found in the daily lives of Simeon, Lucius, Manaen and the rest of that original little band. They took no offices, nor did they esteem one higher than another among themselves. They imposed no structure on the gentile converts. They took no position but, rather, lowered themselves to where the others were. They put a high premium on unity and the Lord's will rather than their own. *This* set the standard for everyone else's attitude toward one another. As far as the gentiles knew, to be a Christian was to be like Simeon, Lucius, and Manaen.

Don't misunderstand, there were administrative matters in the church, lots of them. But the unity of the body was so unbroken it appears that administration was taken care of by everyone. What was left over was probably shoved off on someone in the original band. Assumedly, if anything came up that defied solution, it was dumped in Barnabas' lap. But responsibilities, and who it was that should take care of them, were very fluid and undefined. Primarily the church seemed to move along, taking each week as it came, getting by on unity, love and consensus. Any young church will go through just such a stage as this before it gets elders, but Antioch just never got out of that stage!

Eventually the church in Antioch emerged as a unique blend of Jewish morality without Jewish legalism, and the free, uninhibited nature of the Greek without the typical Greek immorality.

Next, Antioch ended up with some pretty outstanding men.

The church in Antioch started without elders, and seems to have never gotten any. It also started out without prophets or teachers, but later these men did arise. Who were they? You can guess. After about fourteen or fifteen years of church life, Manaen, Lucius, and Simeon were raised up by the Lord to be prophets and teachers. (Barnabas was already recognized as a prophet when he got to Antioch. In fact, Barnabas was considered *extra*-local.) There were other men besides Manaen, Lucius and Simeon who became prophets and teachers, but we do not know their names. So Antioch turned out to be impoverished in elders but rich in prophets and teachers! By the fourth year of the church there apparently were a half dozen or more such men.

It is easy to imagine, then, what the church looked like by the time it was four years old.

There were hundreds of believers.* They lived in clusters and met in homes all over the city. The meetings were purely

---

*It was later estimated that the church in Antioch eventually grew to the point that 20% of the population of the city was following Christ. If that is so, then in the last part of the first century about 100,000 people were in the Antioch church, making it perhaps the largest single church in all history.

gentile. Men were proclaiming the Gospel all over the city. Prophets and teachers were circulating all over town, proclaiming the Gospel out in the open, ministering in the homes, building the church and strengthening the new converts.

One last thing can be said about the church in Antioch. It constantly had the witness of *prayer* before its eyes. There were men in that church who lived before the Lord. Those men constantly testified that their ministry was *first* to Christ and *then* to the church. Take note: the church's foundation rested, not on the shallower foundation of evangelism, but on a very powerful foundation of deep spiritual experience.

The Lord took note of this fact. He chose, one day, to come to five men who were meeting together in prayer to speak to them in a very special way. His word was so significant that we must class that prayer meeting as one of the most important events in all church history.

It was in that meeting the Lord wrote a new page in Apostleship. It was in that meeting the destiny of western man was fully altered.

Let's go join that prayer meeting.

28

Apostles Number Fourteen and Fifteen

It is late winter. The year is 47 a.d.

It is one of the great moments in human history.

Five Antioch men have decided to spend the day together in prayer. But this will be no typical prayer meeting. There will be no pleading, no begging, no intercession. This is a special kind of day, a special kind of prayer. Five men will be *ministering to the Lord!*

Ever since those gentiles were converted in Caesarea, the Lord has been nudging history in a new direction. Today, in this prayer meeting, that redirection will be completed. Of course, the five men who have come together don't know this. Nonetheless, all future generations will have to return to Antioch, to this room, to these five men and to this prayer meeting to discover what caused the greatest turn in the history of western man.

Lucius, Manaen, Simeon, Saul and Barnabas were the men present.

What happened?

God broke into history.

Sometime during the meeting, probably toward evening, a most wondrous thing took place: The Holy Spirit spoke individually to every man present.

Now, is that possible?

Yes, it certainly is.

Can five different men individually hear the voice of the Lord... with no human influence? Can all of them receive *exactly* the same word?

There's nothing to it: all you need is the experience these five men have had in encountering the Lord.

If you don't understand the full meaning of that statement, just look at the lives of these men.

They are *not* young. They are not impressionable new converts, not pawns being maneuvered by someone older than they, *telling* them they heard the Lord speak.

Then what kind of men are they, that they *hear* the voice of the Lord? Well, on one hand, they are not super-special. They are not Apostles; but neither are they neophytes. They are typical, but mature, Christians—five local men who are prophets and teachers in the Antioch church. All of them are very responsible. No one stands above the others in spiritual stature; they are equals. They are honest, sincere, mature, experienced, no-nonsense Christians. . . and they *all* heard the voice of the Holy Spirit.

Let's take a closer look at these men because their testimony, "We *heard* the Holy Spirit speak," has altered the lives of almost every man who has lived on this earth since that century. Let's see if *we* can trust them.

Saul is the youngest man present; *he* is around thirty-nine! Saul has been a Christian for the shortest period of time, *ten* years. He has been in church life for four years.

Barnabas is forty-seven. He has been a Christian seventeen years. Four years ago, at the end of thirteen years of being a Christian, Barnabas became a worker in the Lord's Kingdom.

Simeon, Manaean and Lucius have been Christians for well over a decade and have known church life for seventeen years. About a year ago (probably) Simeon, Manaen, and Lucius were raised up as local prophets and teachers *in* the church in Antioch.

A pretty formidable group.

It was these men who laid claim to having heard! To such men as these the Holy Spirit dared to entrust His word. To these men God gave a higher revelation of Himself, His ways and His work! Why God chose these particular men, we don't know. All we know is that He judged them to be trustable.

How did the Holy Spirit speak to these men corporately? Consider your own experience. At some time in your life you have undoubtedly heard the Lord speak to you, have you not? You *knew* it was the Lord. Perhaps you had a personal problem. Then the Lord clearly spoke.

What happened in Antioch was similar to your experience, yet with a difference. In this case the Holy Spirit spoke separately to five men; but it was the *same* word! He didn't speak to them about some personal problem, however. He was speaking about heavenly matters, about God's work. He spoke about His Son, and His church and about taking *them* to the whole world.

Such a corporate speaking of God only happens in the church, and even then, rarely, and only to men deeply rooted in spiritual encounters.

Spiritual history was written when that word was given! Just look at the new thing that happened as a result of that speaking.

The *first* was this: the *Holy Spirit* spoke!

And He gave a command. It was the type of command that, until then, only the Father and the Son had ever given. Today God introduced a new way to commission Apostles, a way never before used by a triune God!

The Father had once commissioned *an* Apostle. The Son had once commissioned *twelve* Apostles, but never before had the Spirit sent out *any* Apostles!

The *second* historical note is *what* the Holy Spirit said.

The Holy Spirit told five men to set aside two of the men present!

The task? To take the Gospel to the whole gentile world. That is, to take a Hebrew experience to a non-Hebrew planet!

That brings us to history-maker number *three*. In this simple command, God was turning *two* men in that room into *Apostles!* Now that is amazing. Why? Because until today there had been only twelve such creatures in the whole world. The Holy Spirit's words clearly showed that God intended to have *more* than just twelve Apostles! Probably no one had ever dreamed of such a thought.

And these two men had their own unique sending ... completely different from the sending the twelve received. You will recall that the first commission had been given to *twelve* men by *Jesus.* The Lord had actually said, "You twelve will be witnesses unto me to the uttermost parts of the earth." The twelve had always assumed that prediction (for it was a prediction, *not* a command)* meant they would take the Gospel all over the earth to all the *Jews.*

This second commission, given today in Antioch, was given not by Jesus, but by the *Holy Spirit,* and it was a clarification of that first commission. Today God was saying: "Take the Gospel to the whole world." Period!

The Lord was completely unshackling the Gospel from the Jewish religion. The Gospel was now for *all* men, for the whole world; it could be taken even to places where no Jews lived! *The Lord had launched the evangelization of the world in earnest!* God had opened every city on earth to the church! The Gospel of the Kingdom would at last have the chance to be heard everywhere.

Truly this was a historic day.

That's not all. In the near future, as a result of this day, the Lord would give a new way of raising up churches; and He would give it, not in Jerusalem and not in Judea, but in far flung places like Galatia and south-eastern Europe.

Looking back, a few years after this prayer meeting, men came to realize what a spectacular thing God had done. He once sent *twelve* men to the *Jews.* But today, the Spirit, in unprecedented action, had commissioned Apostles numbers fourteen and fifteen to take the Gospel and the church to the whole *gentile* world!

Fifteen Apostles? Yes, fifteen.

Let's go back at this point and look at the lives of these first fifteen Apostles. Let's see the whole process God used to make them Apostles. It is an important process to see. Why? Because we need Apostles again. Desperately! We have soul

*Most people understand the Great Commission as having been given to all Christians. It was not. It was given exclusively to twelve men. Most Christians think of the Great Commission as a command: "Go ye into all the world." That is not correct. Jesus was only letting them in on the future fact that someday they would go. "You shall be going" is what He *really* said.

Sorry about that!

winners. We have pews. We have steeples. We have organizations. But not *Apostles!*

Men win lost souls easily enough: that doesn't take either depth, consecration or power. Men raise up religious organizations easily enough: a new one is born every day. That only takes organizational ability, promotional power and a vision with a verse of Scripture to justify it.

What about raising up churches?

Nothing to it. Men do it every day. (At least they think they do.)

All you need to "raise up the church" in our age is a building, a steeple, stained glass windows, pews, and a group of people who agree to show up every Sunday morning at 11:00 a.m. Oh yes, and you need a can of paint . . . to paint the word "church" on the front of the building!

That may be a church as modern man understands it. But it is not the church *as it was first experienced.* Why isn't there something like the early church on the earth today? The reason is simple: it takes a certain type of man to produce *that!* We need, therefore, to see how God raised up those first fifteen Apostles.

There were several traits common to the lives of each of these fifteen men. For instance, all fifteen, at one time or other had been *called.* Called? Yes. They heard a call from God previous to their sending. This was true even in the life of the very first Apostle, the Lord Jesus.

Jesus Christ was *called by His Father* before the foundation of the world, called to be the first Apostle, called to build the church. (The church, the bride, was literally taken out of His side, just as Eve was taken out of Adam's side.) Jesus Christ *authored* the church; *He* built the church.

What about the second group of Apostles, the twelve? Were they also called?

Along the blue shores of Galilee the twelve were *called* to be Apostles by the Lord Jesus.

God the *Father* called Jesus Christ to be an Apostle. God the *Son* called the twelve to be Apostles.

What of Barnabas?

We do not know anything about his call, we only know, by the testimony of the Holy Spirit, that he had been called. But when, where, we don't know. It is never mentioned in any of the ancient records. He was probably called in Jerusalem during the time he became aware that God wanted a higher expression of the church than Jerusalem. It may even have been that Barnabas did not recognize his call as a call. Not at first. Sometimes it takes the passing of years and a look back to understand these things clearly.

And Saul?

Saul was converted to Christ on a trip to Damascus. He was also *called* that very same day!

So, in Apostleship, there is first the call. Many, many men today have been called. There are thousands of men God has called to minister in His Kingdom. But in our age men have the *call* all mixed up with the *sending*. God never sends men who have been called until they have survived (yes, *survived*) the second step, the stage of *preparation!*

To be called is not a license to *serve*.

A man who has been called but not sent is easy to spot. It seems he is *always* getting some kind of a call. He is called as a pastor from one church to another. Or he is called to be on staff with a religious organization. *Then* he is called to the campus. *Then* he is called to work with businessmen. *Then* he is called to launch his own religious organization.

He is always being called. He is always moving. He is always changing locations, seeing a broader vision, joining (or starting) a *new* movement. And, if you look closely, things like climate, money, prestige and problems seem to influence his hearing the new call.

A *sent* man? He has been sent to build the church (not the "universal" one either). That's his only job. Come the whole alphabet, from *a*valanches to Zulus, nothing will stop him, for the church will be his whole life. Why? Because he has seen the church, been in it, and he has a sending: a sending that is too real, too overpowering to ever be distracted by lesser things.

The sent man, *a result of church experience,* lives only for the church. He is blind to all else.

You can judge for yourself about how many of the Lord's servants have been *sent.*

Let's move now to the *preparation* for Apostleship, and let us look at the first Apostle, first. Did you realize that Jesus Christ went through a period of preparation to become an Apostle?

In the days of Jesus Christ a Jew who wished to serve the Lord did so by first receiving training in the priesthood. When a young man reached the age of twenty-one he actually left home, moved to Jerusalem and began his preparation so that one day he could serve in the temple. He was trained for *nine* years—from age twenty-one to age thirty.

The Lord, at the age of twenty-one was a carpenter in Nazareth! Nine years later, when his peers had finished their preparation they entered the priestly ministry.

And so did Jesus Christ!

Who got the better preparation, the thirty year old priest in Jerusalem or the thirty year old carpenter in Nazareth?

You know!

Well, what exactly was the preparation God gave the Lord Jesus? The answer is important. After all *He* is our standard of what a servant of God is to be. Furthermore, He undoubtedly got the most thorough preparation God ever put anyone through.

Look at the preparation of Jesus Christ.

For one thing, His preparation was hidden; His life was wasted. Jesus Christ wasted the best decade of His life, age twenty to thirty. (He should have been out there winning souls; everybody knows that.)

What did He learn during those hidden years? Perhaps you never thought of this, but He learned to be *human.* He had never been a human before, He had only been God. Now, by first-hand, on-the-job experience, He actually entered the arena of mankind and there learned humanity.

That is not all.

Under His Father He learned humility; He learned submission; and by that submission He *won* authority. He learned suffering, patience, waiting. He learned to live perfectly and constantly in His Father's presence.

He fellowshipped with the Father. That fellowship between those two was, in fact, *the beginning seed of Church life!*

There was more to the Lord's preparation than this, more than you and I will ever know, but this is enough to give you an impression.

One thing is clear, *God reckoned this simple preparation of His Son, a carpenter, hidden away in a little country town, to be a far better preparation for Apostleship than was the temple seminary in Jerusalem!*

What of the preparation of the *twelve*?

Right after the twelve were called in Galilee, they began living with Jesus Christ. And they continued to live with Him for nearly four years. That was the most important part of their preparation, *to be with Him.*

The next order of business was the Lord's demand for *the loss of all things*! They left the influence of all other kingdoms and came under the pull of His alone.

And more!

During those four years they lived in the constant presence of the Lord. During those sacred years, twelve men learned God. They *watched* divine Life! They ate with it, slept with it, talked to it, observed it, touched it—in every possible situation, under all possible circumstances! They handled the very life of God. Constantly. His presence was always there.

Next?

They learned the way He thought; they learned His relationship to the Father. They had a ringside seat to see Jesus Christ live the Christian life! They *observed* the secret of the victorious Life!

There was more.

They got exposed. Oh! Did they get exposed. For four years their weaknesses, their hidden motives, their corrupt hearts, their worldly ambitions, their total lack of spiritual insight, the shallowness of their lives, their utter refusal to really suffer, all of it came to the Light. Such corruption is in all of *us*. The difference with the twelve is that *they* got *caught!*

They were exposed!

They fought with one another, got their feelings hurt, pouted, argued, resented, gossiped about one another. Eventually, though, the exposure took its toll; they lost their false faces. It took years to get really exposed. It always does. But finally they even got down to being human. *They,* like their Lord, learned true *humanity!*

They finally gave up any thoughts of superiority or "specialness" and learned to accept themselves and one another as a hopeless mess. It was out of this exposure, this knowledge that they were utter failures, that there began to grow up on earth man's first experience in church life.

Twelve men built together. Twelve men always with Christ. Twelve men living directly under the Lord's headship. On dusty, lonely Galilean roads, Christ and the twelve, together. Packed into a living room, sitting around a seashore fire in the evening, on board ship, bedding down under Judean stars, always together. These conditions brought forth a unique relationship among the twelve; and among the twelve with Christ.

The lifestyle that developed between twelve men and Christ was, in fact, the first experience of church life man ever had. In fact, *the church in Jerusalem was modeled* after the relationship of the twelve living with Christ!

But let's go on, for there is more.

Mark this. The four years these twelve men spent with Christ were four wasted years! They did virtually nothing! Jesus never expected them to do anything. You just can't find full time Christian service here. Christian service cannot be justified on the basis of their lives. In fact, out of about 1,200 days the twelve spent with Christ, they engaged in "service" for only fourteen!

Get around *that*!

There is one other ingredient in the preparation of the twelve Apostles. It was something very important, yet it is an element that has been largely overlooked.

The twelve got to see the Body function exactly as it ought to function! They saw every office which God planned to have in the church. They saw every gift expressed exactly as it should be.

How is that?

The church would one day have prophets. While the twelve were living with Christ they saw what a *prophet* was. They also saw what an *evangelist* was. They watched the greatest of all evangelists! They were prepared to recognize the true gift of *teaching* on the day when that gift would appear in other men. How? They heard the true teacher teaching.

They also watched a *deacon* serve, for Jesus Christ served them. They learned how *administration* was to be handled in the church, for they saw Him administer. They knew how to recognize the true gift of *benevolence,* for over and over again they watched Him give. They also lived with the first *elder* the church ever had! They understood eldership. They knew how purely a man should handle the gift of *discernment.* How did they know? Because *they had watched Him,* and His way, in the function of discernment.

Over the course of nearly four years, they saw them all: every function, every office, every gift to be known by the future church. Each was *first* exhibited *by the Lord!* And the twelve saw! They saw. One day these functions would live in them and, on a day still further in the future, in other men. And the Twelve would be able to tell if the gift in a man was really the Lord, or just *almost* the Lord!

Perhaps the most important lesson they learned was in seeing how the one in charge relates to those in his charge. In the Lord's presence, right in front of Him, those twelve men made an awesome number of mistakes (enough mistakes to have been rebuked a hundred times), racked up an incredible number of sins (enough to have been excommunicated from the church a dozen times), and broke a hundred spiritual principles (enough to disqualify them all from *ever* being servants of God); yet they saw how He treated them, despite their horrible score! That altered them. The twelve would always remember the love and acceptance with which they were treated; it profoundly affected the way they later treated others in the church. And those in the church were profoundly affected by the tender handling of the Apostles.

That, in turn, affected the way everyone else treated one another.

Awesome, isn't it?!

This was how divine conduct was introduced to earth. It was introduced by Jesus Christ in His treatment of the twelve men. Divine conduct was lived out in a *man,* in front of other men . . . by means of divine life.

Finally, the day came when the Lord took His nature, His character, His disposition, His gifts, His conduct, His higher life form, and planted them in the twelve. All that He was came to live in them. The twelve, in turn, living by the same Higher Life, properly exercised these gifts before the church in Jerusalem. The church, in turn, got to see the authentic use of each divine gift. The church watched the gifts operating. They noted the modesty, humility, hiddenness, tenderness, compassion, and patience.

They watched divine life live itself out in men!

Then it was the twelve's turn to watch again.

Praise God, they lived long enough to see these same gifts arise in the church. The twelve got to see the Lord manifest His own Life and gifts in *young* men. They immediately recognized what they saw . . . as being the Lord Himself!

There was one final element to the preparation of the twelve: they experienced the *cross.* They took the full brunt of the cross and were utterly broken under its impact. They learned humiliation. They knew the bitterness and joy of repentance and forgiveness.

Still later, beyond the cross, they experienced the *resurrection.* And, a short time thereafter, they were *empowered!*

All this happened from 27 a.d. to 30 a.d.

This is how *they* were prepared for Apostleship!

It is interesting that *Barnabas'* preparation was very similar to that of the twelve.

As already noted, Barnabas was in Jerusalem from the very *beginning* of the church, just as the twelve followed the Lord from the very beginning of His ministry. Also, like the

Lord and the twelve, Barnabas went through a long period of wasted years. He did not serve the Lord for the first eight years of his Christian life. (Or was it thirteen?) He, too, had his day of exposure, humiliation and trial. He learned submission to authority. He gave up everything. In fact, three times he abandoned his home to follow the Lord's onward move, first in the year 30, then in the year 38, and again in 47 a.d. He learned that following the Lord was a lifetime commitment to having nothing and going anywhere.

Barnabas sat for about a decade, just watching the twelve, as *they* had watched the Lord. He watched those twelve men function in the role of evangelists, prophets, teachers. He watched how beautifully they administered the every day details of the church. He saw their limitless patience with the body and its members. He experienced their patience, for it was exercised on *him*. And he remembered later, when he got to Antioch and the full weight of responsibility fell on his shoulders, how he had been dealt with so patiently during his "thickheaded" years.

Barnabas learned well the lesson of submission: submission that is joyous, under authority that is brokenhearted.

In a word, (1) Barnabas learned from the twelve all they learned from Christ, and (2) he drank deeply of the well-springs of the church.

What about *Saul's* preparation?

Saul had been a Christian for ten years when the Holy Spirit made him an Apostle. He had been through two major stages in his Christian life before the day the Holy Spirit made him an Apostle.

The first stage was the time he spent alone in Arabia and then in Tarsus. Those were the wasted years, time just spent getting to know the Lord, living before *Him*, receiving a deep revelation of His nature and learning His ways. That first stage covered six years.

Secondly, Saul spent four years in the church in Antioch. He was in Antioch from the *beginning!* He saw exactly how Barnabas began, how he raised up the church. Then Saul settled down to learn from Barnabas all that Barnabas had learned from the twelve.

By the way, Saul learned church life in one of the most dynamic churches in history.

Now, finally, Saul is going out as an Apostle. Yet, even now he is an apprentice. Notice the order in which the Holy Spirit sends the two men out: "Barnabas and Saul."

All right, we have seen the *call* of Apostles; we have seen the *preparation* of Apostles. Now let us see the most overlooked part: the *SENDING*.

Our whole planet is messed up today because men are confused about their call and their sending. Hundreds of thousands of *called* men are all over the earth at this very minute doing all sorts of things—visionary things, needy things, things they like to do—and are doing them "for the Lord." But none of these men has been *sent*. There is no one doing the *one* thing that God wants.

It is important to understand God's sending. Why? Because being *properly* sent is extinct!

Look at first century sending. Again we must first look at Jesus Christ, because He was the first *"sent one."**

We know the exact spot where Jesus Christ received His sending. It is locatable! The Lord was *sent* by His Father at the Jordan River on the day He met John the Baptist.

And what was His sending?

What was Jesus Christ sent to do? (Certainly not to found a non-profit, tax-exempt, inter-denominational organization!) The Lord came into the world to do many things: for instance, He came to save us from our sins! But He was very specifically *sent* for one thing: *to build the church.*

In that sending God set the standard of true Apostleship for all ages to come. Apostles are sent for one thing and for one thing only: to found, raise up, and build the church. *They have no other task.*

Jesus Christ did not do anything until He was sent. Repeat: He began to serve the Lord *after* He was sent. Before that he did absolutely nothing. Until He was sent, He was being prepared. His life was utterly hidden until that day. Would to God that men would learn His lesson.

*The Greek for "sent one," as you probably know, is Apostolos.

213

That was the first "sending." God the *Father* sent His *Son.*

Now let us look at the second sending.

The second sending was the sending of the twelve. It took place on the Mount of Olives. There Jesus Christ sent twelve men. Then, just a moment after He sent them, He ended His life on earth as an individual. Before their very eyes He ascended to the Heavens.

(By the way, one of the characteristics of *any* Apostle is this: he will eventually, *always,* leave the work he raises up. Jesus Christ was the *first* Apostle to do this. He even said, "It is necessary that I go." It was important that even *His* followers be left alone without His physical presence, so they could come to utterly depend upon the Holy Spirit. A true Apostle will always leave the churches he raises up. He will leave them to the Holy Spirit.)

The Apostles accepted their commission, but for the next nine days, in the company of 108 other people, they prayed and fasted. Then, on the tenth day, they went into the building business! From that day forward the church was their sole obsession.

This was the second sending. God the *Son* sent the *twelve.*

Could there ever be a *third* sending? Could there be a third set of Apostles? It wasn't likely. After all, Jesus Christ was no longer on the earth. Who would prepare them? Who would send them? No one really expected any more Apostles, not after the ascension.

Now you can understand how important that five-man prayer meeting was. It actually happened. Not on the shores of the Jordan River when the Father spoke from Heaven (in 27 a.d.), not on the Mount of Olives when Jesus sent twelve men out (in 30 a.d.). No, this is Antioch. A prayer meeting. The year is 47 a.d. Two new Apostles are added to the work of building churches. And this time, the third time, it is the *church* which has done the *preparing* and God the *Holy Spirit* who is doing the *sending!*

This is revolutionary.

From this day forward, forever, the preparing of Apostles will rest with the church, and the sending of Apostles will be done by the Holy Spirit.

There is one last thing about this day that is remarkable: the *number* of Apostles sent out to evangelize the entire non-Jewish world!

When God looked down on Palestine, with a Jewish population of about one or two million people, He decided to send twelve men. Twelve men to evangelize Palestine. Twelve men to plant a church in almost every city of that country. Seventeen years later when God looked down on the rest of western civilization, the known world,* He sent out *two* men! Two men to reach 250 million people and *thousands* of cities!

Surely our God is not a God who thinks or acts as men do today. He sent two men out to do the job of evangelizing the world! Two men to raise up a testimony of His Kingdom in every city!

Can they do it?

No.

But they will make a pretty good beginning. And they will never once stoop to employing the methods we use in the twentieth century.

(For the record, these two newest Apostles could not have been sent out at a worse time. God often uses bad times and picks poor places, to do His work. For instance, in 30 a.d. He arranged for the church to be born in the one city that hated Jesus Christ the most. Very poor circumstances to begin in. Now the Lord is sending Barnabas and Saul out during the dark hours of an international famine.)

Let us turn now from seeing how God prepared His first fifteen Apostles, and return to that Antioch prayer meeting.

After the Holy Spirit spoke, the five men, surely very excited, called the entire church together and told them what had happened. The church, just as excited, stood utterly with

*The estimated population of the Roman Empire at that time was 250,000,000 people.

215

the word they had received. Once again the five men fasted. Then Manaen, Lucius and Simeon, in the presence of the entire church, laid their hands on the two going out.*

The next few days must have been very busy as the two mapped out their plans. Where would they go? How would they begin?

Let's see.

*The original text is difficult to interpret. It may be the entire church laid hands on Barnabas and Saul.

Books you might like to read

◆ Radical books for radical readers

BEYOND RADICAL

A simple, historical introduction into how we got all of our present-day Christian practices.

You will be thunderstruck to discover that there is really *nothing* we are doing today in our church practice that came directly out of man's determination to be scriptural. Virtually everything we do came into being sometime during church history, after the New Testament. We have spent the rest of our time trying to bend the Scripture to justify the practice.

WHEN THE CHURCH WAS LED *ONLY* BY LAYMEN

The word *elder* appears in the New Testament seventeen times, the word *pastor* appears only once (and nobody knows what that word had reference to, because there is no place in the first-century story in which he is clearly seen).

But there are over one hundred and thirty references from the day of Pentecost forward that refer to either "brothers" or "brothers and the sisters" (Greek: *Adolphus*). *These* were the people who were leading the church. There are only two major players, from a human viewpoint, upon the first-century stage. They are the church planters and God's people—the brothers and the sisters. Everything else is a footnote.

OVERLOOKED CHRISTIANITY

What is the view of the Trinity on these three critical aspects of faith:

1. How to live the Christian life
2. What is "church" really supposed to look like
3. How are workers—specifically *church* planters—supposed to be trained

Revolutionary, radical and arresting! These are the words which best describe this one-of-a-kind book!

Overlooked Christianity makes a great companion book to *Rethinking Elders* and gives clear answers about *what to do* in the practice of our Christian life!

AN OPEN LETTER TO
HOUSE CHURCH LEADERS

A simple statement on what a more primitive expression of the Christian faith should be centering on.

◆ Books which show what the Christian faith was like "first-century style"

REVOLUTION, the Story of the Early Church
THE SILAS DIARY
THE TITUS DIARY
THE TIMOTHY DIARY
PRISCILLA'S DIARY
THE GAIUS DIARY

The story! Perhaps the best way we will ever understand what it was like from the day of Pentecost in 30 A.D. until the close of the first century is simply to know the story. Allow yourself to be treated to, and enthralled by, that story. (Warning: Knowing the story will change your life forever.) You will find that story in every detail, with nothing missing, in these *six* books.

◆ Books which glorify Jesus Christ

THE DIVINE ROMANCE
A book of awe, wonder and beauty.

THE STORY OF MY LIFE AS TOLD BY JESUS CHRIST
Matthew, Mark, Luke and John combined into one complete gospel written in first-person singular.

ACTS IN FIRST-PERSON
Beginning with Acts 1, Peter tells the story of Acts through chapter 11. Then Barnabas, speaking in first person, tells the story of Acts from chapter 13 to chapter 15. You then hear Silas, Timothy and Luke continue the story all the way through, ending with chapter 28.

THE CHRONICLES OF THE DOOR
The record of heaven as told in;
THE BEGINNING
THE ESCAPE
THE BIRTH
THE TRIUMPH
(the resurrection)
THE RETURN

◆ Books which show you how to experience Christ

The following books serve as an introduction to the Deeper Christian Life:

LIVING BY THE HIGHEST LIFE
THE SECRET TO THE CHRISTIAN LIFE
THE INWARD JOURNEY

◆ Books that heal

Here are books that have been used all over the world, and in many languages, to heal Christians from the deep, deep pains they experience as they go through life. Some were written for Christians who have been damaged by their churches and damaged by other Christians. Others are books which help you understand the ways of God as they are now working in your life. All of these books are known and loved around the world.

A TALE OF THREE KINGS

A study in brokenness based on the story of Saul, David and Absalom.

THE PRISONER IN THE THIRD CELL

A study in the mysteries of God's ways, especially when He works contrary to all your understanding and expectations of Him.

CRUCIFIED BY CHRISTIANS

Healing for Christians who have been crucified by other Christians.

LETTERS TO A DEVASTATED CHRISTIAN

This book explores different techniques practiced by Christian groups who demand extreme submission and passivity from their members. It faces the difficult task of dealing with bitterness and resentment and rebuilding of faith and trust.

Contact SeedSowers Publishing House for a catalog of these and other books, including great classics from the past on the deeper Christian life, as well as new publications that will be appearing annually.

SeedSowers
PO Box 285
Sargent, GA 30275
800-228-2665
www.seedsowers.com

SeedSowers

THE WORKS OF T. AUSTIN-SPARKS
The Centrality of Jesus Christ... 19.95
The House of God... 29.95
Ministry.. 29.95
Service.. 19.95

COMFORT AND HEALING
A Tale of Three Kings *(Edwards)*................................... 8.95
The Prisoner in the Third Cell *(Edwards)*..................... 7.95
Letters to a Devastated Christian *(Edwards)*................. 5.95
Healing for those who have been Crucified by Christians *(Edwards)*........ 8.95
Dear Lillian *(Edwards)*... 5.95

OTHER BOOKS ON CHURCH LIFE
Climb the Highest Mountain *(Edwards)*......................... 9.95
The Torch of the Testimony *(Kennedy)*......................... 14.95
The Passing of the Torch *(Chen)*................................... 9.95
Going to Church in the First Century *(Banks)*............... 5.95
When the Church was Young *(Loosley)*......................... 14.95
Church Unity *(Litzman, Nee, Edwards)*......................... 14.95
Let's Return to Christian Unity *(Kurosaki)*................... 14.95

CHRISTIAN LIVING
Final Steps in Christian Maturity *(Guyon)*.................... 12.95
The Key to Triumphant Living *(Taylor)*......................... 9.95
Turkeys and Eagles *(Lord)*... 8.95
Beholding and Becoming *(Coulter)*............................... 8.95
Life's Ultimate Privilege *(Fromke)*............................... 7.00
Unto Full Stature *(Fromke)*.. 7.00
All and Only *(Kilpatrick)*.. 7.95
Adoration *(Kilpatrick)* 8.95
Release of the Spirit *(Nee)* 5.00
Bone of His Bone *(Huegel)* 8.95
Christ as All in All *(Haller)* 9.95

Please write or call for our current catalog:

**SeedSowers
P.O. Box 285
Sargent, GA 30275**

**800-228-2665
www.seedsowers.com**